D0744004

The Jesus In Mary Lou

R. Kyle Chappell

PRESS

www.xulonpress.com

We wish to acknowledge the great number
of people,
who must go unnamed here, who have prayed
for Mary Lou
throughout her life and supported her in the
mission fields of India.
And those who have stood by her during all the
trials and difficulties she has ever faced.
Because of you she has never been alone
or in want.

And all who have gifted their remembrances
and proffered
quotes and given of their time in proofing
and editing and
previewing and endorsing
The Jesus In Mary Lou.

Mary Lou's Mission Statement Verses

"I, the LORD, have called you for a
righteous purpose,
and I will hold you by the hand. I will keep you,
and I make
you a covenant for the people and a light
to the nations,
in order to open blind eyes, to bring out
prisoners from the
dungeon, and those sitting in darkness
from the prison house.
I am Yahweh, that is my name;
I will not give My glory to another or
My praise to idols."
Isaiah 42: 6-8

The Jesus In Mary Lou

Part One: A Thrown Away Child

Part Two: "India! That's The Last Place I Would Go!"

Part Three: You Always Will Have India With You

End Justifies Means

During the Roaring 20's Marie Curie made two trips to tour the United States, where she was welcomed enthusiastically. The Nobel prize laureate had been honored in the fields of physics (1903) and chemistry (1911). Curie's reason for being in America was fund-raising (for research on radium). Marie Curie was an agnostic, her mother a devout Catholic, and her father an atheist.

Marie Curie knew of Henrietta Loucks and of her recently diagnosed cancer. In 1925, intent on the study of such diseases and the effects of radiation upon them, Marie Curie encouraged Henrietta to have a baby.

"To have me as an experiment to see whether cancer was hereditary."

A baby for the sake of science... to be studied... just like the proverbial guinea pig.

Stricken

Marion Louise Loucks was born in Youngtown, Ohio February 13, 1926. A Saturday. At age five she moved with her mother to Buffalo, New York. Henrietta was a patient at Roswell Memorial Hospital where she was one of the first persons ever treated experimentally with radium. Her father, brother and sister followed later in the year.

She was Shirley Temple cute but even as a young girl Marion Louise had quite a deep voice and it seems she just couldn't manage to sit still. Her first doctor, Doctor Miller, called her 'Ferdie The Frog With Ants In Her Pants'. She was called Mary Lou right away by family but not so generally until the advent (reintroduction actually) of a popular song. 'Mary Lou, I Love You' pulsed the airwaves and whenever Mary (not being contrary) Lou heard it she would shout "Me, me, me!"

Her name had been so given that by the first grade, which Mary Lou had just entered, variations were used by the teacher to singly communicate with half a dozen different students. There were Marion, Mary, Mary Lou, Lou, Louise, and Mary Louise. For the record, Mary Lou was Mary Lou. She could easily have been, were a seventh form needed, Mary Lou Lou (in deference to her surname).

Also all the rage... and it certainly seemed to Mary Lou all the other kids had them... were roller skates. Mary Lou "really, really wanted" her own pair and her mother, due the scarcity of money in 1931, purchased the least expensive roller skates available. They were the gift of Mary Lou's fifth birthday. In February in Ohio you didn't necessarily roller skate, so Mary Lou awaited the mobility and the freedom of their use.

When that day came she eagerly rolled down the cobblestone drive. In a devastating instant she caught a wheel and fell; on contact, the cheaply constructed skates disentegrated. The base metal pieces impacted Mary Lou's body in unimaginable ways. The injuries were severe. The muscles of her legs were detached and sharp shards entered her all over.

During the next three plus years she endured thirty-six operations, some minor and some major, to repair her body and, unable to move on her own, was carried everywhere. "I could not even crawl."

There was no provision for her, a crippled child, to attend school and so she did not from age five to age nine. Missing those years led her to study undauntedly on her own. Her only textbook was the 'Human Interest Library', an encyclopedia of twenty-one volumes, from which she learned her fundamentals of math and science and English and history.

Abandoned

Off to an unusual and then harrowingly bumpy beginning one can just imagine the thoughts that could be running through Mary Lou's young mind. But, as the witness to her story will discover, normal responses were just not for our Miss Loucks.

"Most children would have been angry at life and at God at this point. Even though I did not yet know the Lord, I knew He existed. I would pray for strength to get through the day and for God to show me and teach me His ways. It was not easy. Because of my accident, I barely had skin on my legs, you could see my bones."

Adding to their woes, her family was quite poor. Christmas stockings usually held an orange, an apple, a banana, and nuts. Half of these gifts came from their side yard.

In 1935, at age nine, Mary Lou heard a story about Jesus on the radio and in it a person was healed. Mary Lou had been crippled for four years and the thought excited her. "If Jesus is Lord, as they say He is, and God, I want to know Him". Without knowing how to pray she prayed these words: "If You are the Lord and Savior I will follow

You. If it please You I would like to be healed". It's all she said. It was all she needed to say.

"I know some don't believe in healing. I did not go to any tent meetings. No one ever 'laid hands' on me. I was all of a sudden just healed."

Standing itself proved to be a very difficult challenge but within the day she was able to walk. Her first steps were from her bedroom to the family's sitting room. Twenty-five feet. No matter what, now, as promised, she would follow Christ the rest of her life. That was all she needed to do.

"This caused me to have a burning desire to know God. I would study the word. I went to any and all meetings at the church. This great God I heard about had healed me, little insignificant me, whom nobody else seemed to care about or love. Maybe He could love me?"

Her father, her earthly father, was of French-Dutch descent and an atheist. Her father was artistic... winning many awards in display contests... but he had another side, a dark side, that only her family saw. "To the community, he was a nice, friendly man who sold paint. Inside the walls of our home however, he was a different person. He used to abuse me physically. He had a real hatred for me because he never wanted me to be born. He couldn't afford another child and only had me to please my mother. He often took his anger out on me. I can remember him slapping my hand if I touched something I wasn't supposed to. One time in particular, I picked up a glass and he slapped my hand so hard that I dropped it and it broke. Other times he would beat me with a wide, leather, razor-sharpening strap. I had welts on my back until the age of nine."

Her father would have nothing to do with the premise of such a miracle and declared, "God did not heal you! There is no God!". He believed, in utter disregard of the physical evidence before his eyes and all he knew to be true, Mary Lou had been playing a very long game, faking it as if that were possible, and that she could have walked of her own volition at any time previous. So blind and bitter was he, after a few weeks time, he threw his nine year old daughter, in her frail condition, from home and family. He sent her out onto the streets of Buffalo, New York. Cast away, not for being a Christian. Because she wanted to become a Christian.

"Can we follow the Savior far,
who have no wound or scar?"
Amy Carmichael

2525 Delaware Avenue

$\mathcal{D}\mathcal{V}$

A unt Cora Holly and Uncle Dick Holly owned a delicatessen. 'Holly Delicatessen' (which they opened in 1931!). Mary Lou, not even realizing how desperate her situation could prove to be, walked directly there and was providentially, and secretively, taken in. The disowned nine year old was permitted to sleep in the cellar on beer cases (room) and eat leftovers from daily deli preparations which didn't sell (board) in exchange for work. A lot of work. The roar of the furnace just there, so very near her flop, and the tastes and associated smells of the whole of that store linger vividly in Mary Lou's memory to this very day.

And never will her routine be forgotten. Up at four o'clock every morning, to bed at midnight every night. Four hours off for sleep, then twenty hours on for chores and school, then another full round of chores. 20/7. A monumental effort for a young girl. For anyone. Child labor laws were, well, well-intentioned.

"My aunt was nice to me. I still had to work very hard to earn my keep."

Mary Lou made fifteen loaves of bread early each morning (the most elicit smell of all), and

donuts, and cabbage slaw, and potato and mac-
aroni salads, and meatloaf. She did the Holly
cleaning. She swept out the delicatessen and
swept off the sidewalk (and shoveled snow in
season) before heading to school (8:45 to 3:00).
She returned to the store from 12:00 to 1:00 for
lunch. When not otherwise occupied she worked
behind the counter, selling everything in sight.
Much of her studying was done at the cash reg-
ister between sales, where her schoolbooks always
lay open and at the ready. A strong work ethic
became so completely engrained in Mary Lou's
psyche that she continued 20/7 for the next 53
years, through all the years of service in a place
she had yet to even imagine.

She attended the first grade at the age of nine.
Not the usual age of six. In second grade she was
ten. In seventh grade she was fifteen. Not twelve.
She didn't miss any grades but while covering
ground and catching up she was never the typical
age of her classmates. And she was always way
the tallest. Mary Lou graduated high school at 21.

Potentially such a difference could have proved
traumatic for everyone involved. Mary Lou was so
well liked by all, however, that it never became
a problem and Mary Lou was so balanced and
assured she wasn't put off by it. She dated as early
as the fourth grade, always going to the movies.
Sometimes this was with boys her actual age and
sometimes with boys from her actual class. The
fellow who took her to her 8th grade dance is the
man who now grooms supreme court justices for
that position.

After school Mary Lou strode 'home' on the QT
to do her mother's work. Henrietta's cancer had

advanced to the point where she could do little (her arms had to be raised horizontally at all times). For Mary Lou it was laundry (actually taking it back to the delicatessen to do), cleaning again, and cooking again. She prepared the evening meal her father, somehow unaware of its origin, would consume and Mary Lou would not. There was nothing for it though. She had to help her mother... and she did so without fail for four years.

Mary Lou had an older brother, Howard, and an older sister, Claudia. Claudia, in sharp contrast, pretty much refused to help and only chipped in when forced to chip in.

When Mary Lou was at 'home' her mother would sit at the window and watch for the return of her husband. She would warn their daughter and send Mary Lou packing... out the back door to run across the fields and back to Aunt Cora's. Whenever her father occasioned the delicatessen Aunt Cora would likewise signal her to flee. He could never know Mary Lou was ever there for they all knew she would be beaten if found out.

School #81 through the 8th grade was just back of Holly Delicatessen. All of Mary Lou's teachers, she reports, liked her and were very kind to her. Miss King in 1st grade. Miss Fisher in 2nd... Mary Lou's favorite. Miss Hicks in 3rd and 4th. All of her teachers were Misses.

From grade four on, incredibly it seems, Mary Lou was very athletic. She played basketball on school teams all the way through college.

A thin girl through the age of ten Mary Lou now was filling out. Though she worked hard and long and was always active her diet consisted of unsold potato salad and donuts not chosen.

She actually became weighty enough that the other kids, though kids need little impetus, felt compelled to begin calling her "Fat, fat, fat... the baseball bat!". To such terse teasing she had no response. Not because she couldn't think of any... because she already had the ability to let the negative comments of others roll "like water off a duck's back".

'Sticks and stones' were another matter and one physical prank played on Mary Lou at afternoon recess went terribly wrong. Her legs were pulled while swinging and she fell, spread-eagle, hard onto the cinders below. The small rocks cruelly punctured her arms and legs and stomach and face. She was taken inside and stripped naked. They showered her, rubbing most of the stones out... and perhaps a few deeper in. Those imbedded in her knees remain with her today, and she bears the scars to prove it. Even as she recalls this unhappy and painful event Mary Lou giggles nonchalantly. "You accept what happens to you."

Around that same time (two years after her arrival at 2525 Delaware Avenue) Uncle Dick Holly unexpectedly died. A small flat, which he was preparing for himself and Cora, was gradually finished and Mary Lou moved in instead. She had to give up her bedroll on the beer cases and the fiery furnace. There she stayed, in her home away from home, safe and secure from all alarm, and her father, until she left for the far-flung land of India at the ripe old age of 26.

Three Wise Women

A trio of women, Betty Thompson, Mary Finch, and Mrs. Simpson were very influential in Mary Lou's early years. The latter lady, the wife of the doctor who cared for Mary Lou's mother in the cancer research center, picked Mary Lou up in her "big, blue Cadillac" each Sunday and delivered her to North Delaware Methodist Church. "I felt like a queen." This Mrs. Simpson did for seven years, rarely missing a beat. 360 micro-ministries.

Betty Thompson, who lived only two blocks away from Holly Delicatessen, wanted to adopt Mary Lou outright, but could not. She was a teacher to mentally retarded children. Each day, intentionally, she would pass by after school at a predetermined time. Mary Lou would try hard to be outside the store at the very moment to at least be able to exchange a wave.

Mary Finch (while Mary Lou was in India) willed Mary Lou $10,000. She further supported her all of her years in country (and a family trust still supports her to this day). Relatives of Mary Finch would also take Mary Lou to Canada for vacations, to a splendid Keswick Christian camp, and did so frequently. On such outings these folks profoundly affected her spiritual growth. In fact, it was in that second largest country in the world that Mary Lou received her calling to go to the mission field. She was sitting down by the lake, reading her Bible, when she suddenly and strongly felt the Lord's calling. Immediately she knew as well, however these things are known, she had just been called to India. When she related her experience to others she added, "But I'm not going. Not to India."

"Betty Thompson was not married and Mrs. Simpson had no children. The two were good friends and both of them treated me like I was their own daughter. Betty taught me about culture. She took me to operas and other musical programs that I otherwise would never have been introduced to. She also was my Sunday School teacher. Mrs. Simpson would see that I was behaving in church. Both of these ladies encouraged me spiritually."

Others visited Mary Lou at the delicatessen whenever they could, sometimes going well out of their way to do so. Fifteen year old Cleora Keeley (in the mid 40's) rode her Champion bicycle three miles to be able to "chat about everything and solve the world's problems". Seventeen years later Cleora traveled to India to visit Mary Lou. Way out of her way. She got an elephant ride in Gandipur Forest, although without Mary Lou, who was very ill with hepatitus just then. Thirty years after that Cleora met up with Mary Lou in California. To date, a friendship of 65 years.

Higher Education

"It's God that does these things. Only God.
And that's why I don't want people
to think it's me.
It's not me. It's God."
Mary Lou Frederick

From the age of five, back before the skates accident, Mary Lou wanted to be a doctor. She determindedly honed her medical skills by bandaging the legs of tables. And she learned as a small child how to treat the physical manifestations of her mother's raging disease (and the intense radiation burns she received with treatment). Mary Lou was a nurse before she was old enough to start school.

Mary Lou recalls her favorite entry in her Human Interest Library encyclopedia was Abraham Lincoln. Impressed even at that age she was pleased, at the age of eighty-three, to learn Lincoln had once slept at the American Hotel on Main Street, Buffalo, New York. It was 1861 and he was on his way to accept the Presidency.

At Bennett High she excelled in art (her talent had been noticed as early as kindergarten). She painted windows for prize money, always winning it seemed. She went into Teacher's Training after Bennett High and there won five scholarships in competitions which her art teachers had pursued on her behalf (never did she enter a judged contest on her own). At seventeen Mary Lou entered Teacher's College and a year later entered Buffalo Bible College (which is now Houghton College).

At Bennett High Mary Lou once got away with murder. Murder was something uncharacteristic for Mary Lou... so much so her honesty could not even convict her. On a dare from a boy Mary Lou placed slabs of rather exotic cheese (Limburger) on the school radiators. The effective stink resulted in the entire student body being assembled in the auditorium. The guilty party must admit to the crime and accept the punishment.

So Mary Lou, caught and penitent, head bowed, stood up amongst all her peers and teachers and fully confessed.

The school authorities, in response, knowing Mary Lou's reputation quite well, said, "Yeah, right. We know it wasn't you Mary Lou. You may go home."

"While I was at the State Teacher's College I asked the Lord to let me meet some Christians. One day I walked into the school. There were four girls (Dee, Jen, Joy & Lois) sitting on a step and they asked me if I was a Christian. I said 'Yes'. We became lifelong friends and still correspond today. We started prayer meetings and Bible studies at the school. We started with one prayer meeting and Bible study per day, and grew to four prayer meetings and Bible studies per day. We contacted InterVarsity Christian Fellowship nationally and through them we opened up a chapter at our school. Bill Bright, the InterVarsity leader at our school, would later go on to establish Campus Crusade. The InterVarsity Christian Fellowship at the State Teacher's College later spread into the main campus of the University of Buffalo."

"While I was at the Bible Institute, I heard a great missionary come to speak. It was my now late husband Edward Frederick. He was not my husband then. He gave a sermon about being unequally yoked to nonbelievers. At that time, I was engaged to a nonbeliever. After the sermon that day, in my next two classes, both of my professors spoke on the same passage of scripture! Well, I was so convicted from this, I knew the Lord was speaking to me. I went home and broke off the engagement. Little did I know that the speaker whose words I obeyed was the same man I would marry almost four decades later!"

At twenty-two (fresh out of high school and after being called to the mission field) Mary Lou switched from Teacher's Training to Nurse's Training, thinking it would most likely serve her better in any coming ministry.

Aunt Cora Holly, showing some true colors, would not pay any expenses because she did not want Mary Lou to be a missionary and Mary Lou had "not one red cent" to pay the cost of Nurse's Training... the day before she was to travel to New York City to attend. That evening a group of about forty people met at her church for prayer and to send her off and say their goodbyes. Traditionally at such gatherings gifts of clothes and similar necessaries were bestowed. A woman stood, and then one person after another stood, saying the Lord had indicated to them they should give a gift of money on this occasion instead. Enough was collected in that manner, in that hour, to exactly cover Mary Lou's $1,000 tuition, the train fare from Buffalo to New York, 10 cents to get her from the train to the hospital on the subway, and 3 cents to buy a stamp to send a thank you to the people for the money! Exactly.

I know what you are thinking. Exactly?

Exactly.

Mary Lou received no additional funding for six months and providentially her new room and board was included in the price of tuition.

She made and painted plaster of paris boats and did oil paintings and sold them to pay extra expenses but rarely could she go out with others to get pizza or join in any girl games. She would excuse herself by telling them she couldn't go "because I have to study because I have to get straight A's." She knew God would supply anything she really ever needed. She had known this all along. But, socially, it was a dry spell in wants due to her oh so tight finances.

Jesus replied to them, "Have faith in God.
I assure you:
If anyone says to this mountain, 'Be lifted up
and thrown into the sea,'
and does not doubt in his heart, but believes
that what he says
will happen, it will be done for him. Therefore,
I tell you,

all the things you pray and ask for—
believe that you have
received them, and you will have them."
Mark 11:22-24

Throughout her education, she is first to admit, "I was not a good student. I would pray and God would answer."

And, doing her part, she studied extra hard to get her marks. At first she was not going to be accepted into Nurse's Training... but they looked to her grades and decided Mary Lou was diligent in her efforts and worthy of admission.

She prayed "God, if you want me to be a nurse, open the right doors. If not, close them."

"I then applied to three separate nursing schools and got into all three even though I did not pass any of the entrance exams. I was not a brilliant student, but I was a hard worker. They saw my good grades in high school and college. When they asked on the application: "Why do you want to go into Nurse's Training?" I answered, "Because I need discipline. I want to be a missionary nurse."

"So I began my studies at the Methodist Hospital (in Brooklyn). Lights out was at 10 p.m. so I used to sit out in the hallway and study longer by the hall light. The subjects did not come to me easily. I really had to study for them. Many times, my hands on, practical work came easier for me. I especially had to learn how to spell, it was my worst subject."

(Editor's Note: Mary Lou's spelling gene never did quite kick in so it was one discipline she would never fully master. Too busy was Mary Lou with more important matters.)

Often it seemed Mary Lou Loucks was a sore thumb roundhead in a community of status quo squareheads. She just stuck out.

"I used to get in trouble and get sent down to the office of the Director of Nurses. You were not supposed to fraternize with people above or below you. One time I got into trouble for going out to church with a dietician. I would also get into trouble for talking to the sweepers, and custodians, or for opening doors for people who were under me, and for smiling too much!!! When they asked me why I did what I did, I would simply reply, 'Well, I told you on my application that I needed discipline. I've been my own boss since I was nine.'"

"Another time I witnessed to a patient who was Roman Catholic and she became a believer in Jesus. When this happened another nurse who was also Roman Catholic got upset. I got sent down to the office again. This time I told them 'you can't get me in trouble for this because I told you on my application, before you accepted me, that I was entering nurse's training to learn how to be a missionary nurse. I even wrote that my mission before going would be to the patients, fellow students, and the staff.'"

Then came an undeniable display of divine intervention. When Mary Lou wanted to go for her RN (Registered Nurse, not Royal Navy) the Director of Nurses, Mrs. Anna Bentley, was strongly opposed and was not going to let her take the State Boards. She said flatly and authoritatively

Mary Lou would "in no way" be able to pass them. That it would be a mistake to even try.

Mary Lou then revealed to the Director of Nurses and 'the other powers that be' that God had promised her she would pass. And because of this Mary Lou as much as guaranteed her success. Though unanimously unconvinced, they relented.

When the test results came in Mrs. Anna Bentley wrote Mary Lou. To inform Mary Lou "You got the highest marks in all New York State!"

1952
Sixty-Second Annual Commencement
Exercises of the Methodist Hospital of Brooklyn School Of Nursing
Monday evening, May Fifth Nineteen Fifty-Two Eight O'clock
All Saints Church Seventh Avenue and Seventh Street Brooklyn, New York
Hicks, Emily Joan
Howell, Norma Janie
Loucks, Marion Louise
Manuel, Georgina Ruth
Martin, Muriel Joan

Salvation's Song

J esus always has known Mary Lou was His. It was a particular joy for this writer to learn that the final single prompting... the last bit in the mosaic of Mary Lou's salvation story... was the singing of "At Calvary" (by an opera singer). A long time personal favorite. "Years I spent in vanity and pride, caring not my Lord was crucified, knowing not it was for me He died..."

Mary Lou was thirteen. After 'leaving home' she longed for something meaningful and secure. She sought Jesus. She first went to the synagogue... and found it did not satisfy her need. She visited a Catholic church which her brother Howard attended... to find nothing to quench her thirst. "And then one day I heard children singing in a Daily Vacation Bible School about Jesus." Mary Lou walked straightway over and asked if she could join them. This was the North Delaware Methodist Church. There were answers there to her wonderings.

She had no parental guidance. She had been on her own for four years... pretty much her own boss... living with guardians and angels. Within weeks Britain and France would declare against

Germany and the world would live another hor-
rific war. The career of Bonnie and Clyde had just
ended. The Lindbergh kidnapping was sad history. It was the year Mary Lou's mother died of
cancer. And Mary Lou met the Lord amidst the
verses of a hymn written in 1895 she herself had
sung many times before. That night, that occasion, its words, its message, really sunk in. Later,
alone, she knelt at her bed and prayed "Please
come into my life."

"And He did."

Was then her burdened soul found liberty.

"I sought the LORD, and He answered me and
delivered me
from all my fears. Those who look to Him
are radiant
with joy; their faces will never be ashamed."
Psalm 34:4-5

On A Wing And A Prayer

To India by boat. Embarking on the Cunard White Star Line M. V. 'Britannic'. The winter of 1952. New York to Southampton in 'missionary' class. Southampton, by train, to London. London, on a second passenger liner, the Strathnaver, to Bombay. A month-long journey and an adventure of a lifetime.

A friend, dockside at departure, later wrote: "When we arrived they would not let us on the ship. We spotted Mary Lou and the rest of the party (five in all) leaning over the rail. She was waving and smiling in a certain direction so we walked down the dock and found some of her friends. Excitement was high... and sadness too. Mary Lou looked older to us. We kept waving to her and finally she spotted us and waved back. The gangplank was removed and two tugs steamed up alongside and moved the ship slowly out. People stood crying. One woman had to leave the rail she was crying so hard. Mary Lou watched us all the time, and we all kept waving back and forth until we could not make out anyone on board."

New York to Southampton. "We are nearing the end of our second day on the high seas. It has been rather rough and most of my time has been spent in the bunk. I have only tossed my cookies once for which I thank the Lord. I really don't know whether I am sea sick or if it a reaction from my yellow fever shot or the cold I have. Probably a mixture of the three."

London. "While Bob, Frank and Carolyn looked around in a second hand store Milton and I went to the London Bible Society and bought our Bibles in the language we are to someday speak. On the way we saw many of the old streets of London and also many of the war torn areas. We got our tickets for the Strathnaver and on our way back we stopped to see an exhibition on India. From there we went to the Wax Works (again) and in the afternoon we went to an excellent exhibition on the Holy Lands."

London to Bombay. "Thursday we dashed to the train and it took us right to the ship. After we got on board we settled our cabin and made it look a little homey and then we had life drill. On deck for this we met Dr. Martin, a missionary in northern India, going back for her third term."

"We were feeling a little out of place now, in first cabin quarters, but there was not much we could do about it. We sure don't have the clothes to keep up with them but praise the Lord our clothes don't matter."

"We walked around the deck and enjoyed the sunset, the moon and the stars. They were just so beautiful that one could not begin to describe them. After breakfast we viewed the cliffs of Spain. The sun beat on them so that they varied in color from the darkest browns to red and then purple. On the very top of one cliff was a lighthouse standing in majestic glory. I am sorry I did not bring my oil paints along."

"We held Sunday School in the afternoon and I was given the privilege of teaching nine year old boys and girls. There were twelve in my class and every one of them knew the way of salvation and their knowledge of the Bible was amazing. I asked how many of them regularly attended Sunday School and they all did but one. When I asked her where she learned the truths of the Bible she said 'school'. That was a public school in England. That sure puts America to shame. This not only gave us a real opportunity among the children but also the parents, as I had six in this class, and the Staff Commander of the Strathnaver."

"We docked at Port Said for a few hours. A typical Egyptian city. At a temple the men (from the tiniest boys to the old, old men) were having their prayers and worship. We also saw Mohammedan Egyptian women. Dressed in black, faces covered. We also saw a funeral. The mourners lined up in the balcony and watched, prayed, and wept. It was a pitiful sight and again we longed to give these people so steeped in heathenism the message of salvation."

"We are going through the Suez Canal. The moon and stars are shining so brightly. As we look toward land in the moonlight it looks like great sheets of snow... but it is the desert sands. Occasionally you can see the low tents of the nomads or a village of one story flat-roofed houses or a small oasis where the shepherds are gathered with a flock of sheep."

Mary Lou left for the mission fields of India without any promise of support. Her passage and

meals on board were paid... and that was that.
She had zero financial provision. Faith was her
springboard. The prayers of people escorted her
across the Atlantic. She believed unhesitantly
that she had been called of God to go and that He
would cover every need.

"Taste and see that the LORD is good.
How happy is the man who takes refuge in Him!
Fear the LORD, you His saints, for those who
fear Him lack nothing.
Young lions, lack food and go hungry,
but those who
seek the LORD will not lack any good thing."
Psalm 34:8-10

Missions today does not convey that God will
keep His promise to meet needs. It's not even a
line item on the spreadsheet. Mary Lou's encouragement is "Just go!"

Mary Lou was joined by three men and one
other woman, her missionary shipmates. Caroline
Strable, Bob Crow, Milton Rust, and Frank Wigg.
All from India Mission... on the way to different
mission fields in India. On the Britannic Mary
Lou offered Bible studies to the shipbound MK's
and non-MK's, of which there were many, and the
gather-ups were eagerly attended. Who knows
what wonders were wrought in the minds of these
children? Instead of video games and computers
they had images of Jesus dancing in their heads.

The five adults also held Bible studies of their
own, led by Bob Crow.

"Mary Louise Loucks, R. N., formerly of 2525 Delaware Avenue, and a member of the North Delaware Methodist Church is now serving the Lord in Chitaldroog, Mysore State, India as a missionary nurse. She is a graduate of Grade School No. 81, Bennet High School, The Buffalo Bible Institute, and the Methodist Hospital in Brooklyn, New York. During her residence in Buffalo, she was an active worker in the North Delaware Church teaching Sunday School, Youth Meetings, Pioneer Girls, and Daily Vacation Bible School. Since she is serving under the auspices of the North Delaware Church (and The India Mission) the church has planned a very interesting program built around their 'First Missionary'. This meeting is open to the public and interested friends, and includes many musical numbers as well as a tape recorded farewell message to the church and the reading of many interesting letters written enroute."

(Editor's Note: Today Mumbai, formerly Bombay, is the capital of the state of Maharashtra, with a population of 14,000,000, ranking it as one of the largest cities in the world.)

Mary Lou arrived in Bombay January 3, 1953. She was almost 27. Bombay, as they say, was a real city and her first impression of Bombay was instant... the overwhelming chaos and vast numbers of people collectively adding to the fray. She was struck and fascinated by everything she saw as she traveled from that coastal city to Surcundrabad.

"The Strathnaver docked early in the morning but due to passport inspection, filling out papers for permanent residency, etc., we were not off the ship until after 1:00 in the afternoon. We were helped through customs. My custom fees amounted to 308 rupees. By the time we were all finished it was after 4:00 so we took taxis to the Salvation Army Hotel. After freshing up we had tea and then went on a two hour walk around Bombay. The people all just stared at us as we did them."

"As we traveled along (by train) there were many stops and at each stop there would be all ages of children from those just learning to walk to children of about ten and twelve crying out 'boc-shees', which means give me something. There were mothers with a baby on their hip crying the same and all kinds of crippled and blind. It was just pitiful. It made your heart ache and to think we could not even give them a tract or speak to them about the Lord. It made me want to get to Chitaldrug all the faster and learn the language."

"We saw many little villages on the plains. They were of two kinds. One of small huts made of anything the people could find... rags, goat skins, cardboard. Usually ten to twenty homes with fifty to a hundred people around them. Another would be larger and also have a lot of houses made of clay bricks. All the villages were near, or had in them, beautiful temples and animals roaming about. The women would be grinding, carrying wood, weaving, washing clothes, or making bricks while the men would stand around or sit nearby watching. Children of all ages would also be doing work."

"Crop fields are vast, with the majorty being rice. You often see idols that they worship, and miniature temples, right there in the fields. For irrigation water buffalo pull up a large bag (made of buffalo skins) of water from a well which is released to flow down an incline to the fields. It is a very picturesque scene."

"It is fascinating to see the people carry bundles, water pitchers, baskets, etc., on their heads without touching them and without them falling off."

"You go up the street and you see a lot of rickety old buildings that look as if they are going to fall apart any minute. As you draw closer you see these are their shops. What are those black things on the counter? Pick one up. Surprise. The flies come off and we see they are an Indian delicacy fried in gia (fat). There are dates and figs. Let's have some. Oh! No. One of our missionaries, not from our mission, died just a few months ago from eating bad figs and dates. Magazines and papers... most of them Communistic. Let us see what a chemist shop is like. They carry all kinds of medicines, some of which you've never heard. The shop is very cluttered and the chemist does not know one medicine from the other. If you don't know your medicines don't buy any as they will give you anything just to sell you something. Your medicine could be water."

Chitaldrug, Mysore State, India. "I really have been kept busy. The day after arriving (January 8th) I began work in our dispensary. The first taste of our work and I really saw the spiritual needs of these people as well as their physical needs."

Mary Lou's first living quarters were in a church... a church with no name. It was simply church. And it was where she opened the smaller of the two dispensaries she manned in India. And then she stayed with a family for six months. "Mr. and Mrs. Fedricks (sic) and their 5 little girls ages from 1 1/2 to 10 gave me a very warm welcome and have taken me into their home and family. So you see that I am now Aunt Mary, and they keep me busy, but I love them."

"Our first dispensary was in a church in the town of Chitaldrug (in Mysore State). I dispensed drugs and did lots of lab technician work there three days a week with my language teacher, Mr. Danials, interpreting for me."

"After several years we moved about seven and a half miles out of Chitaldrug. We had found out that the government had built five houses in the country, hoping to get water from the lake to the area. At first they were willing to give them to us, but we offered rent because we did not want to be obliged to the government. They rented them to us for ten American dollars ($2 per house)! At this new dispensary we were able to set up two wards for overnight patients, a lab, a ward for outpatients, and a house for ourselves."

In the 80's all who came to the dispensary were introduced to the Gospel from a tape recorded message blaring out of Mary Lou's bedroom window (she did play it unabashedly loud). And, as often as humanly possible, they heard the Good News from Mary Lou herself and her helper Prammama.

"I will praise the LORD at all times;
His praise will
always be on my lips. I will boast in the LORD;
the humble will hear and be glad.
Proclaim with me the LORD's greatness;
let us exalt his name together."
Psalm 34:1-3

She had been cautioned about traditional Indian food. Eat small curried portions and she would gradually get used to the heat. So, when visiting, and she was always offered much (as was the custom), she took little. Not once did she get blisters in her mouth. Her favorite Indian cuisine: chicken curry.

Thirty-six years hence, at Christian Fellowship Baptist Church, Mary Lou would attempt to recreate the ambiance, the character, and atmosphere of India she experienced daily so folks stateside could dare to live it for a few moments. In a worthy effort she came close but, if you haven't been there... well, you haven't been there.

India Itself

Contrasts and extremes.
"The land of smells, yells, and bells."
And mindboggling activity and overly burdened streets. People, bicycles, taxis, dogs, buses, cars, cows, carts, merchants, beggars, thieves, oh, my. And contrasts galore. And extremes aplenty. Aromas and noises and sights... many good ones and all the bad ones. And some you would never consider possible.

And hundreds of millions of people living closely with untold individuals in abject poverty, locked there by failed government efforts, an ascetic culture, permissive beliefs, and caste.

And a few living in great wealth (in sight of the poor).

And space. Over a million square miles of it (the U.S. is only 3X India's size) making it the 7th largest country in the world.

And yet crowdedness. 944 people per square mile. Eleven times that of the U. S.

And other numbers which stagger. That's over a billion people. A thousand million. With a baby born just about every second.

There is no word in Indian for the word privacy and the concept of it is pretty much unknown in country (a very collectivest culture).

Relationship is key. Hospitality is paramount.

Yet female infanticide still takes place. And dowry deaths often occur (in-laws kill a new bride if they decide her dowry is not acceptable).

Contrasts and extremes.

Language Barriers

"At Babel, God created an extremely effective
barrier to separate people.
It takes God-sized help to overcome it."
Dave Schoch (missionary to Albania 1996-date)

C hallenges aren't little obstacles... they're the
big ones. And some challenges are bigger
than others.

The four missionaries Mary Lou journeyed
with to India all knew German. They had picked
it up in their youth and now they would learn
Kanarese from their German textbooks. German
to Kanarese. A singular challenge in itself, but it
was they who had an edge. Mary Lou, growing
up, was not allowed to learn German. Henrietta,
her mother, was Jewish, and so it had been for-
bidden. As a consequence Mary Lou would now
have to learn two extremely dissimilar languages
simultaneously. English to German to Kanarese.

(Editor's Note: Kanarese is the local language
used around Kanataka, India, which today some
38,000,000 people speak. It is one of over 400
living languages in country.)

She had a language tutor but Mary Lou was pretty much left to educate herself once again. She had to be very self-motivated. Her two methods were private study and community practice. She spoke often to the children passing by in her fledgling Kanarese. If they laughed at her she knew she had made a mistake(s). She fortunately had the ability to laugh along with them and if asked Mary Lou will tell you humor is a favorable companion on the road of language acquisition.

"I have an hour with my tutor, four hours of study, then another hour with my tutor, and then two more hours of study (8 hours daily). I have been given all the vowels and 13 consonants plus 50 words of vocabulary... all in just one hour. Please pray for me."

"This language is very hard. It being a musical language (you knowing my lack of talent in music) might help you to understand why I am having such a problem. However, our Lord has promised an ear to hear and a tongue to speak."

Still every tongue or dialect she learned was with difficulty. Later, by trial and error and sheer, practical effort, she would communicate in eight languages. In some well enough to give medical instruction to professionals and speak at the commencements of universities.

English, German, Kanarese, Hindi, Telugu, Tamil, Punjabi, Tribal Bataka.

Enough said.

Ophidiophobia

She had been thinking Afghanistan and Alaska (nothing out of the A's) when God clearly called Mary Lou to go to India. Her immediate reply was "No! I won't go to India because of the snakes! That's the last place I would go!"

Maybe God didn't take too kindly to Mary Lou stating her emphatic negative to His country of choice because in no uncertain terms that was where He was going to have her. But then He also knew she would come around. One of the perks of being God.

So, when she eventually said "Yes", after a time of heart wrestling and final conviction, there was only one thing for her to do. Mary Lou frequented the Buffalo Zoo. More than bison, exhibited there also were a wide variety of captivating reptiles. She paid admission in order to just, "Sit and watch the snakes... and throw up". 'India Or Bust' - whatever it took to prepare for future saurian encounters which surely were to come.

And come they did. Once in the form of a "ten to twelve foot, thin, white snake" which coiled up in the red roof tiles of her bedroom ceiling. "I was laying on the floor in my bedroom thinking I would relax a couple of minutes before returning to the dispensary. When just above me what should appear? A snake. I quickly got help but the men were not successful at killing it. When I returned later there it was just as pleased as punch on the rafter above the head of my bed." There was mosquito netting over the sleeping quarters proper but it was not intended to protect against such a weighty creature if it suddenly chose to drop. Mary Lou experimented with sleeping arrangements elsewhere in the house for ten days or so while the snake sojourned.

Once in the form of a small, but quite lethal, viper. One of the 'Big Four' species responsible for the greatest number of human deaths in South Asia (they usually are stepped on and then strike). Mary Lou was standing in the front door frame of her house. She does not recall whether she was coming or going. The viper was poised on the top edge of the door itself and as it moved Mary Lou's roommate, Ruby Enns, inside the house, saw it. She held a small knife. Reflexively and wordlessly Ruby flung the utensil at the snake... and hit it!... knocking it away! A shot in ten thousand.

Together the two excited ladies put the snake out of their misery, whacking it multiple times with a stick. Once dispatched Mary Lou allowed Ruby to see to the burial. "At the time we didn't know what type of snake it was but when we asked the Indian people they were horrified. It seems that if it bites you swell and become all green then die in 15 minutes. The dying wouldn't be so bad as I would be with our Lord in Glory but I don't like snakes and prefer not to be bit by one."

1956. "Saturday I had a visitor in the dispensary. A very beautiful one but not very welcomed. Just as I got to the door that leads to the porch a 4' cobra looked me in the face. I didn't take long getting out the back door. I went around and watched it come in the dispensary and go directly to the place where I had been sitting then out the back door. I would have liked the skin but the people burned it. Well maybe next time."

"The other night a 7' python was killed not too far from here. As this was just a baby one we are still looking for the mother and the father. Personally I do not relish the thought of meeting up with them but we have the great consolation that our Lord takes care of us and if perchance we should get coiled and smothered by one we would know our Lord permitted it and had purpose in it."

Other kinds of animals were encountered which were no less entertaining. There were wild elephants running down main street, which Mary Lou avoided, and domesticated elephants, which Mary Lou rode upon many times. In fact she accompanied great numbers of other missionaries and visitors on their elephant ride. She even took a turn round the jungle (circa 1970) with the future queen of Denmark, Princess Margrethe.

There were close encounters with Black Bear "which most people don't even realize exist in India" and "a close brush with a Bengal Tiger within the first three days of arriving in country".

1971. "While driving we saw a leopard. It was laying in the road, with the car lights on it. We watched for about five minutes and then turned off the lights. It then walked within two yards of us. We turned the lights back on. It sat and looked at us and then turned and walked into the jungle and we went on. We also saw 9 wild elephant, deer, wild boar, and of course all kinds of monkeys."

"Everything looks so dry and parched. We are in great need of rain out here or the famine conditions will get worse. One cannot help wonder if this is God's punishment on this nation where so much food is wasted by the monkeys stealing it and yet they won't kill the monkeys. The need of food and yet they won't slaughter the cows for meat."

1953-1955

7 00 letters written from India by Mary Lou to family members (most to Aunt Lucille and Uncle Curtis Loucks) were 'discovered' recently in a vintage suitcase. They had been kept "as a kind of diary". Dated 1953-1970 they have added much content to this manuscript. Excerpts most remarkable. Other years follow in four chapters.

"Oh that the people at home might learn that they by their prayers can move the Arm of Omnipotence and do more for the work here than we can."

"As you might have heard the people here name you after they get to know you. Sometimes years pass by before you find out what your name is. However we have found mine out. The children let it slip one day when I was walking with about thirty of them. It is 'Crciooo' and is pronounced 'Upacara', which means kindness. This name most likely has been given because I give aid to the sick."

"This past Friday a mother brought in her one and a half year old baby boy. She came from one of the larger villages near Vigapura. The baby had unusual second and third degree burns on various parts of his body. We asked the mother how he was burned. She said they were made by the people of her village by heating glass bangles red hot and burning the child with them. When we asked her why this was done she replied that the baby had fits and they wanted to cure it. The Hindu priest had told them to do so to drive the evil spirits away."

"We spent the last ten weeks in the beautiful Nilgiri Hills (seven thousand feet above sea level) as it was too hot to continue language study on the plains."

"Ruby came down with the mumps and is in quarantine for fourteen days. The Frederick family were on tour so as soon as they got back they went to the hills so they would not have to be in quarantine."

"As God has met my needs abundantly above all I could ask or think, often without a mention of them to anyone, I rather hesitate in writing such a letter. Many people have written, however, asking about specific needs. I can well understand this and appreciate their thoughtfulness."

"The running of the compound has been laid upon me. Quite a bit of responsibility plus work with Kanarese make my days rather full. Our Lord gives the strength and the experience is good so I do not mind. In fact I am rather enjoying it."

"Today I taught Sunday School in a Tamel village. We met in a little room and there were over sixty boys and girls in ragged clothes, hair messed up, and as dirty as you could find them. They listened with such interest and sang so lustily."

"The train was very crowded and I know what they mean when they say 'squashed like sardines'.

The compartment I went in was supposed to seat 16 and over 27 were in it plus everyone's baggage and bedding rolls. No room for feet. We squeezed together a bit tighter so two little girls could lie down. People sit in the window sills with their legs hanging out. And even hang on the outside of the train. I was supposed to have a reserved seat, ha!"

"The other day I had a little girl of five in. Both of her feet were burned severely, one right down to the bones. They are so poor they can't get an Indian doctor so I just have to do the best I can. They left her in that condition for five days because they didn't want to pay an anna (which is less than one cent) to have her treated here."

"We make our bread... a simple procedure in the States, but not here. First we buy wheat then winnow it. Fortunately there is a mill nearby. We bring back 'additional material' in the flour so we sift it several times to remove the dirt and bugs. Yeast was sent from the States (we must make yeast from bananas if we don't have American yeast)."

"Ugowde Festival is over today. It is the Hindu New Year. All the people have their homes white-washed and wear new clothes. On New Year's morning they decorate their doors with fresh mango leaves. Each person takes an oil bath. There are special foods for a feast. They eat the bloom of the bavan flower which comes from the sacred tree which they worship. The people feel that if they eat this blossom they will have peace through the next year. There are many beggars at this time and people do not refuse them. Gambling games are placed along the streets and in all the temples and the majority of the men and boys participate. No matter how young a boy is he may gamble. This play is very riotous and can even be deadly. We have seen some of the most wicked ways of Satan and have seen his bands make these people rage."

"You know in India the boys and girls just talk whenever they want and shout out. They also leave whenever they feel like it. I praise our Lord that all through the entire Sunday School they sat quietly... so much so you could have heard a pin drop. And no one walked out."

"I had a little baby with kidney trouble. It's body was so swollen that the skin broke all over. Full of sores and infection. I treated it for a long time but the baby got worse. I told the parents it was doubtful that the baby would live and asked them if I could pray for the child. Being Mohammedan we thought they would say no but they consented. As I prayed I had Ruthamana interpret so the people would know what we were praying. Asking our Lord to save this child only if it would mean the salvation of souls, especially this family. The baby began to show improvement. Yesterday when the mother brought the baby she was just all smiles. She said she believed in Jesus and that Jesus had healed her baby. It was true. The swelling was gone and the sores all healed but one little one."

"Now this is for you folks only as stories grow if they get around and become a hundred times worse than they were. This past Friday I took Ruby to the Mysore hospital where she had an appendectomy. She was doing fine and had good care so I started home. We often travel at night as it is much cooler and easier on us. Well, two fellows tried to rob me. All they got away with was my glasses and we are praising our Lord it was just that and that they didn't do any harm to me. I was suspicious of them the moment I entered the train and I tried to tip off the guard but he was not on the ball. Afterwards I was well guarded with policemen the rest of my journey."

"For three days and nights the drums have been beating. From my window I can see the large bonfires with the devil dancers dancing around them. Festival drums are beating loud, people are screaming. Horrible to see and hear."

"Most of the people who come to the dispensary are in some way affected with venereal disease. Many of the children are covered with ulcers and their eyes are inflamed. Many come with wounds from falls or from cutting themselves in their religious beliefs. They become worse because they have been treated with the discharge of animals or by the witch doctors."

"We have received our first tape recording from Mary Lou Loucks in India. History is being made for this is the first we have heard of a missionary being in direct communication with the folks at home through tape recordings."

From an early (the name was still India Mission) information flier on India:

"There are about 9 missionaries per million people, and many of those 9 preach 'a gospel that is not the Gospel', or do other work, rather than effective soul-winning."

"India's population is over 400 million—greater than the populations of North America, South America, and Africa *combined!*"

"640,000 villages are without one resident Christian!"

"It is estimated that less than 400 missionaries are free for evangelism in all of India!"

"Do you care? Are you obeying our Lord's command to pray for more laborers?"

"90% of the people live in the villages. 70% of the missionaries work in the cities!"

"About 30,000 people die every day in India without Christ!"

**At School #81 at age 10 in 2nd grade.
Being oldest, Mary Lou is also tallest. She
remembers 7 of the other 9 kids.**

**Nurse Mary Lou just prior to leaving
for India (1951).**

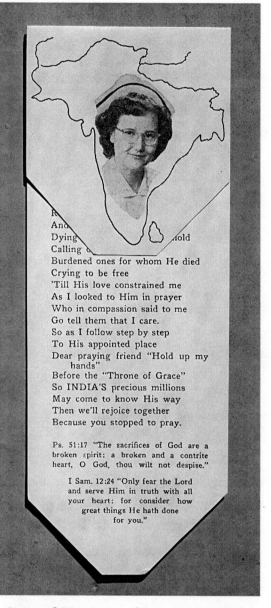

And
Dying   old
Calling
Burdened ones for whom He died
Crying to be free
'Till His love constrained me
As I looked to Him in prayer
Who in compassion said to me
Go tell them that I care.
So as I follow step by step
To His appointed place
Dear praying friend "Hold up my
   hands"
Before the "Throne of Grace"
So INDIA'S precious millions
May come to know His way
Then we'll rejoice together
Because you stopped to pray.

Ps. 51:17 "The sacrifices of God are a
broken spirit: a broken and a contrite
heart, O God, thou wilt not despise."

I Sam. 12:24 "Only fear the Lord
and serve Him in truth with all
your heart: for consider how
great things He hath done
for you."

One of Mary Lou's prayer cards (in the form of a bookmark).

**Taken 1960ish while on one of her rare
furloughs to the States.**

**Another of Mary Lou's prayer cards. This
Bible study was with three of her best nurses.**

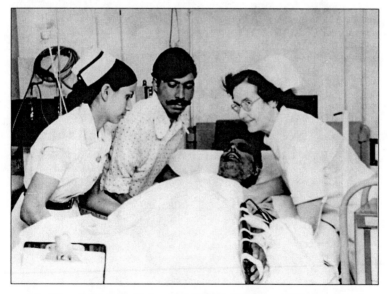

**At the hospital in Ludiana where Mary Lou
set up a cardiac care unit.**

Mary Lou with 7 of the 8 MacLeods (and Indian helpers) before they left Chitaldrug and Mary Lou's TLC. That's the vehicle which crashed (repaired).

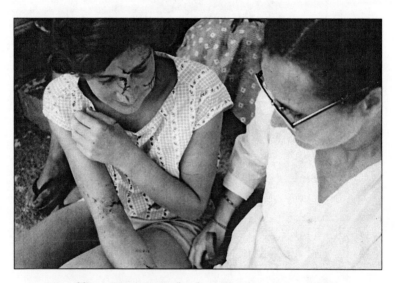

**Marilyn MacLeod showing some of her
injuries. 144 stitches to her face alone. Her
life had been saved.**

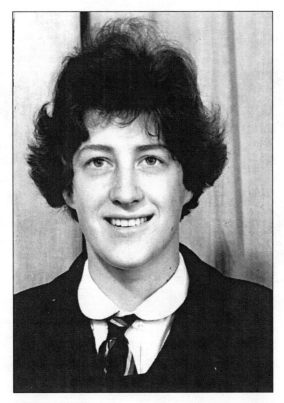

**Miss MacLeod shortly afterward,
showing no scar tissue whatsoever.**

Nothing Sacred

*"If someone were to ask me what
the most important
outward manifestation of Hinduism was, I would
suggest that it was the idea of cow protection."*
Mahatma Gandhi

The one thing, while driving in India, you don't want to do is hit a cow. It is as taboo as taboo can be. Missing them all all the time is not easy, however, because in India big cities have tens of thousands roaming freely about, wherever they please. You do have to miss them all all the time.

One day driving, while in India, Mary Lou hit a cow. A small cow, but a cow nonetheless. Not yet streetwise it mindlessly ran out onto the road and was broadsided. At that point most people would have gone into hiding. Not Mary Lou.

The poor creature did not appear to be badly injured but Mary Lou, though she did not have knowledge of how critical her course of action would prove to be, by herself, loaded the little heifer into the back seat of her '25 Ford. Together they drove 135 miles to Bangalore and the nearest veterinarian just because she felt the animal should be checked out. It was the right thing to do.

After his examination the veterinarian gave the bovine a verbal clean bill of health. That was good to hear but then and there Mary Lou was prompted to request a written and signed clean bill of health... and one was collected. She paid for services rendered, accepted help getting the cow back in the '25 Ford, and backtracked the 135 miles to return the cow to it's rightful owner, who, by zealous neighbors, had been informed of Mary Lou's initial misdeed.

Now flash forward twelve or so years. That same cow, much larger and much older and probably streetwise, becomes ill. It doesn't die... it just becomes sick. Analyzing the situation, and not giving undue attention to any concept of reality, the rightful owner threatens to take Mary Lou to court. It would be okay to settle out of court for a proper reparation in rupees but if not he is willing to sue Mary Lou for the damage she had done to his animal those dozen years earlier... the old bump that undoubtedly had finally forced the beast off its feed.

Probably the rightful owner would have petitioned a winning case, under Indian law, and could have tallied a tidy sum... had Mary Lou not had a get out of jail free card. She kept the veterinarian's note over the decade plus and still had it in hand for show and tell. This realized, the rightful owner's compensation bubble was burst.

India. Driving. Cows. "You can't be too careful."

'25 Ford incidental: This vehicle was originally shipped over the big pond and first owned by Mr. Opper, the first General Director of 'India Mission'.

It was secondarily owned by Mr. Frederick, the second General Director. It was thirdly owned by our Mary Lou Loucks so it was widely rumored she would become the third General Director, which she did not. She did however sell the '25 Ford in the '70s, though it half century old, because it had been fitted for rough terrain and was yet running. Mary Lou's main ride? An Italian Lambretta. A scooter which served her well on the dry, dusty, bumpy, dirt roads of India.

Worst Case Scenarios

"There is always the danger that we may
just do the work for
the sake of the work. This is where the respect
and the love
and the devotion come in - that we do it to God,
to Christ,
and that's why we try to do it as beautifully
as possible."
Mother Teresa

Mary Lou's first dispensary was small and lightly equipped. She set it up from scratch in about two weeks within her church. Her very first patient was seen during the very first day of preparation. Family members brought in a baby boy with sores and blisters and bleeding "from head to toe". The cause of the lesions was unknown but she treated the child carefully and as knowledgeably as she could. Her medicine (penicillin ointment and sulphanilomide powder) worked wonders and the relatives of the baby boy, considering her a miracle worker, became longtime friends with Mary Lou.

Since she was the entire medical staff, and always on call, Mary Lou had to diagnose everything that came her way... all that was recognizable. When she diagnosed cancers she would try to send the patients on to the state hospitals. Usually they would not go. Some did and later the doctors would ask Mary Lou how she knew it was cancer. "I learned it from my mother and I just can tell" would be her plain truth answer.

Bacterium were a huge concern and cholera and typhoid outbreaks were a constant alarm. Leprosy was commonly seen, and its victims, sleeping, were often chewed on painlessly by the nocturnal rat population. It was the way they lost fingers and toes.

A second dispensary was larger, gratefully, and more thoroughly supplied. It consisted of those five small houses built by the Indian government which Indian people never occupied. In years following vast numbers of patients crossed their thresholds and respect for this dispensary became widespread.

It was not uncommon for Mary Lou to see thirty or forty patients each day. And, though not common, she treated as many as two hundred.

Some patients did wish to pay extra in currency for their care but Mary Lou never accepted such money in her ministry. She did take grains and vegetables and, yes, chickens. Some Hindus actually tithed to the dispensary from their family crops.

After those first years in the dispensaries, Mary Lou moved her operations to the Kotagiri Medical Fellowship Hospital, a Christian hospital. It was there she became Nurse Superintendent and began to teach eye training and vaccuum extractors to nurses and doctors. She also began to do more surgeries at KMFH.

"While I was at Kotagiri I was invited to come and work for a month at the Amy Carmichael Place (the Dohnavur Fellowship in Tamil Nadu, 30 miles inland from the south). I had always wanted to visit her sanctuary so I gladly went."

"One can give without loving, but
one cannot love without giving."
Amy Carmichael (in India 1895-1951,
never returned to Ireland)

"Before my time at Kotagiri I joined the ENFI, the Evangelical Nurse's Fellowship of India. I was invited to their camps to speak about the Lord. I would teach Bible classes and seminars. We had seminars all over India for the nurses to teach them about Christ (which was ENFI's main goal). They were widely attended and many nurses accepted the Gospel. There were between 90 and 200 nurses usually. They came from all the different states in India and even from Nepal. We trained them to start up Bible studies in each of their respective states. We went to different hospitals and established Bible studies and trained nurses to teach Bible."

"I enjoyed my time at Kotagiri. While I was there I gained much experience in surgery and teaching. Dr. Paul allowed me to assist him in surgery. We had many patients here with tuberculosis, heart trouble, and jaundice. Seeing the great need that there was for heart specialists, I developed a growing interest in cardiology, which I would later pursue."

When given choice Mary Lou intentionally, purposefully, chose to work on the more difficult cases. To treat the people with the most extensive medical problems. To capture notoriety? Well, no. For the sake of profit? Not a chance. To amplify credit, to improve her resume'? Not this Mary Lou. Give up?

She did so because she knew she would see more of them after the fact. Spend more time with them with follow-up care... so she could share the Gospel message with them... over and over if necessary. It was a trick of Mary Lou's trade.

1956-1958

"We too are much in prayer concerning the Billy Graham meetings. I would hate to criticize a man our Lord is using. Since being on the field I feel that one is treading on dangerous ground to criticize as our Lord can use whom He chooses even if we don't agree with all they do or say. We will only know when we are in Glory."

"He just pulled all her bottom teeth one after another without waiting a minute. The poor woman nearly died of shock."

"When I was down in Hyderabad it took 13 hours to go 120 miles."

"In this vast area we are only five women. Two from Canada, two from America, and one from Scotland. There are the many patients, the teaching of children, visitation in the villages, supervision of the church, and care of the house and dispensary itself. We remember that God loves to use the weak things and the things that in the eyes of men are of little worth, and we believe that if you will support us by prayer there is no limit to His power. We long to see the Cross lifted up and the Lord glorified in this land."

"The dispensary continues to keep busy. We are reaching many new villages. In the one year and eight months that we have been here we have had well over 10,000 different patients and many of them have been here many times."

"Joan got malaria again after the baby came so I have been taking care of her and the baby plus (the first week) seeing from 130-150 patients each day except Sunday and (the second week) 150-200 patients every day except Sunday."

"The drums have been beating all day and will most likely continue throughout the night. Right now there are three devil dancers in front of our house. Crowds of peple are thronged around them. They are yelling and every once in a while you hear the heathenish yell of the devil dancers. Some of the children are on the sidelines immitating them. Oh, what a bond Satan has on these people. A few days back some little children were playing near the church door step. They had a small idol they had decorated like the people decorate the large ones they carry around the streets. One of the boys was carrying it on his head and all the other children were making all kinds of noises. When I came up the children said it was god. I stopped to tell them of Jesus, the only true God. They listened with interest. This story was not new to all the children because some attend our Sunday school. But these children see these idols carried through the streets and worshipped by the people. They come right out and bow down and give offerings to them. It is all they know. Often the children are permitted to stay up late to see the idol processions. Those who go to school daily have to do worship (puja) to idols. Is it no wonder that these little children have to hear the Gospel over and over again before it makes an imprint on their minds?"

"A short time ago a little boy of nine years came for medicine. He had all the signs of malaria. Before this this boy was one of the healthiest in the village. The next day we went out to visit and the boy's brother came and said Rogapa's fever was very high. A few hours later some other children came and said Rogapa was dead. Immediately we went to the home. As we approached we saw the boy lying in front covered with a blanket and the parents leaning over him yelling the most heathenish screams. The week before the father of the lad had taken the leading part in one of the most heathenish of festivals. Before he died his older brother, who is about eleven, would not listen to the Gospel. Now Durgapa eagerly listens and is continually asking questions about Jesus. Also he tells the people of the village that his brother has gone to be with Jesus in heaven and that he is happy there. Many other boys and girls of that village have become very interested in the Gospel of Jesus Christ."

"Once a year the religious teacher (guru) rides around Chitaldrug on elephants in a big procession. He lives in a mansion just outside of Chitaldrug. Many people worship this guru and during the procession give him thousands of rupees. Yet the people are starving."

The Hand Of God

"Expect great things from God;
attempt great things for God."
William Carey (in India from 1793 to 1834)

Instantly... ready or not... Mary Lou had patients and was handling medical procedures normally carried out by doctors. There really wasn't any choice in the matter since there was no one else to do the work. She was the medical team and the work was plentiful.

Mary Lou did skin wounds (and even skin grafts). Amputations of fingers and toes and hands and feet. She did bowel resections. Took out tonsils. Took out appendix. She did what she could for everyone who came her way. And she made house calls. "Sometimes I had to walk ten miles one way to see a patient. I didn't want to be gone from the dispensary for that long but I had to do it."

In a country with many inhabitants living in extreme survival mode Mary Lou at times witnesssed injuries intentionally inflicted. Sadly, who you were could determine your physical condition and future role.

"Often, if a baby were a girl, the family would blind them or break their arms and legs or starve them to use them for begging."

One of the worst cases she remembers... and how could one forget... was that of a young Indian girl with small pox who had been set too near a fire and became very badly burned. Mary Lou treated her burns with cloth that was soaked in tea. "I did a lot of things others did not do." She also used penicillin ointment and sulfnilamide powder spread on cloth to battle eczema... a remedy not then written in the medical books.

One day a man came in who had been attacked by a bear. The brute had bitten the man across his face, so severely that Mary Lou wanted him to go directly to the hospital. The man spoke well enough, however, to say "No, I would rather go home and die." So Mary Lou did her best to sew him up, especially about his mouth. While being repaired he was told about the true God, Jesus. Thereafter, it was confirmed, he never worshipped idols again.

And at times Mary Lou did what she could not do. She would kneel and pray to God for advice. For skill she had yet to master. For knowledge she did not possess.

In 1963, during Mary Lou's tenth year in India practice, she alone faced her toughest day. A nearly unthinkable scenario.

A New Zealand family, both parents and their six children, were traversing India. They rode in an army van which had been converted into a travel trailer. On the rough roads of Bangalore metal fatigued and an axle broke. The MacLeod family careened uncontrollably down into a twenty foot deep trench. Injuries the eight received ranged from negligible to life threatening.

The eldest daughter, Marilyn, age sixteen, had been ejected through the front windshield. "Her stomach was thrown open and her intestines were standing out." One hundred and forty-four stitches were required to close the wounds to her face alone. Above her left eye and forehead. Fully down her nose. From ear to nose across her left check. Her right arm and wrist were gashed as well.

All was done by the light of kerosene lamps. In the midst of what surely would panic most Mary Lou had to be calm and extremely careful with her sewing so the young girl would not bear great scars.

A sister, two years younger, had lost her vision. Had been blinded. There was no obvious cause and Mary Lou did not know what she should do for her so she prayed, asking God to direct her. "He told me to make a little cut behind the brain with a scalpel and take forceps up under the skull and pinch and pull." Not fully understanding, Mary Lou did as directed, making the incision at the optic nerve, and got out "a large clot of blood." And the fourteen year old's eyesight immediately returned.

The mother, herself uninjured, had gone into shock. The father had struck his head on impact and Mary Lou stitched him as well. One son, age six, had received only a moderate cut to his arm. "What was wrong was I gave him penicillin and he was allergic to penicillin. In their state the family had failed to tell me this." To her knees once more she asked that the boy not have a reaction then. And he didn't.

Mary Lou watched over and cared for the MacLeods for two weeks following their accident before sending them on their way. They returned to India to visit Mary Lou several times and sent her flowers each year on the anniversary of their rescue. Flowers to the nurse who doctored them and kept their extreme day from being much more tragic. Of course Mary Lou was not alone in the keeping at all. God was assisting.

Amazingly too, the local Indian people helped to transport the New Zealanders and manually hauled the MacLeod's vehicle up out of the ditch. They brought food for them. They did not steal anything. "Everything was returned to the family!"

The MacLeods wrote their story in its entirety and their account was published in 'The Mission Challenge Magazine'.

March/April 1967. "The New Zealand family will be here till the 3rd. Seven of the eight have come. The eldest girl has stayed home to go to the university. My hands have been full but I have enjoyed having them. They still have not yielded to the Lord and neglect to give the Lord glory for what He did for them on their last trip. They need much prayer. Two of the girls would like to come out and stay with me. One for a year and one for three months. Tomorrow I will take them up to the jungles for an elephant ride and to see wild game. I will be happy to have some quiet time after 17 days of chaos."

Mary Lou traveled to New Zealand herself the year following the accident at the request of the family and the New Zealand government. A full month in Dunedin, she stayed with other friends and also with all eight MacLeods for several days. "They told me they had seen a doctor in Scotland. He asked who did the work on their daughter's face, who went through the windshield. They told him it was a nurse in India. He said this is better than any surgeon had ever done. She has no scarred tissue today."

"After the accident I spoke to the family about my Lord and Savior Jesus Christ. They listened and when I visited them later in New Zealand the whole family had become Christians and were attending church."

On the back of a wallet sized photo still in Mary Lou's possession (a photo showing a girl with a full smile and flawless complexion) is this message: "Dear Mary Lou, I am in great debt to you for mending me up and having such tender care in bathing my cuts etc. I hope you will accept my sincere thank you. In the future I hope you prosper and continue to live a long and healthy life. Love, Marilyn MacLeod."

Supernatural

"First of all, praise God for what He has done in this area. He has given us the friendship and help of the Hindu officials. Given us the joy of seeing many of our patients, whom we thought beyond all human aid, recover because our Lord, who is the Great Physician, touched them and healed them. Our equipment is pitifully inadequate and medicines run out occasionally but God blesses what we use and we stand back and see Him work. These dear people are His patients. All this work is His. To Him be all the glory."

A middle-aged Indian man, carried forty miles by friends and family, was brought to Mary Lou for treatment. He was inflicted with an open throat, as if it had been slit. The actual cause could not be determined from what Mary Lou was told or could tell. Another of the myriad mystery diseases which plagued India (and plague India today)? An attempted murder? A failed suicide?

This man with the open throat could speak, though barely. How he came to the realization was not known but he feebly uttered "I know your God can heal me." He spoke it in his native Kanataka, one of the dialects Mary Lou understood. As soon as she heard his statement she knew the man would be healed.

His injury was three days old and his people said he had just regained conciousness. The trachea was cut partly and the esophagus was cut into. The jugular vein was severed. He had lost a lot of blood and should have had a transfusion and intravenious feeding. Mary Lou did what she could. She cleaned the wound, dressed it, and gave him a shot of penicillin, and then prayed. "All I could do was pray our Lord would overrule."

Then she told the man to return to the dispensary with the same persons with him that day three days hence. They did so and were fairly shocked when Mary Lou removed his neck bandages. Not only had the man's open throat healed... there was not even a mark. No sign at all of a scar.

"This poor man cried, and the LORD heard
him and saved him from all his troubles.
The angel of the LORD encamps around those
who fear Him, and rescues them."
Psalm 34:6-7

1962

"Today I had a letter from my second grade teacher and she sent along a picture that she took of 10 of us in her class. I remembered 7 out of the 9. It was really fun to see."

Excerpts from circa 1962 tourist guidebooks. "Mysore State: It has an attraction for everybody, be he a holidaying tourist, scientist in quest of truth, merchant and industrialist eager on expansion, pilgrim striving for spiritual acquisition, artist thirsting for beauty, or a student seeking unfailing fountains of knowledge."

"It is as though nature and man have conspired together to make Mysore what it is - paradise for visitors. The State is an enchanting land abounding in scenic beauty, rich in flora and fauna. It radiates with eye-some temples and carvings - history depicted in stone by the master hands and minds of old. It has the pomp and pageantry, miracles of modern engineering and abundant gifts of nature. Here, both the ancient and the modern are blended into one thrilling harmonious whole!"

"The fauna of the forest is as rich as the flora. Herds of roaming elephants, bisons, spotted deer and a rich variety of the feathered beings add alluring richness to the green wilds."

"The river Sharavathi cascades into a rocky chasm of 960 feet in depth. The water rolls down in four distinct cascades (Raja, Roarer, Rocket, Rani) presenting a scene of transcendent grandeur and sublimity."

"The Mysoreans have been great empire builders, skilled architects, gifted writers and profound thinkers. Their hospitality and tolerance are well-known. They have received and given shelter to people belonging to different religions."

Up In Arms

"It is a generally accepted fact that the #1 (true) cause for
attrition among missionaries is conflict with other missionaries.
God's Word calls us to love one another but Satan loves to
attack missionaries particularly in this point - after all,
if we are fighting with one another then we are not able to
do the task God has given us.
Unity is a gift from God received through prayer and humility."
Peter Bowers (missionary to the Balkans 1996-date)

It is a baneful commentary that ministries do go awry due to pride. Self-importance of the ministers themselves can and sometimes does trump reason and thus kill a mission. Some missionaries leave the field. Collateral damage is all too often done.

1954. "Since being on the field I have just praised our Lord over and over again for putting me in this mission as it is like one big family. There doesn't seem to be the back-biting, etc., that is found in many missions and everyone wants to help each other.

It is true I haven't been on all our stations but down here the love of the Lord abounds."

1957. "The church in Chitaldrug has been in charge of our missionaries for seven years. As is usual when a real work of God is being done there was a difference of opinion, and a division. The missionaries have tried to maintain an open mind and friendship with both sections, knowing that in such cases one side seldom has the monopoly of goodness. We have been praying that God by His Holy Spirit would deal with the people and lead them to confess their sins to Him and to one another, so that the odium that has been brought on the name of Christ might be removed and the people around see 'the brethren dwelling together in unity'. The most potent weapon the Devil has for bringing reproach on the name of Christ is our disunity, and multiplicity of sects."

Mary Lou, being medical, was typically looked to first and foremost by the Indian people... and not all her teammates appreciated this in a positive way. In fact such natural response from the Indians caused enough friction that two new colleagues and her own roommate (the very one who saved Mary Lou from the snake) chose to report Mary Lou to International Missions as the inciter of trouble. They wrote of her attempts to steal their fire. Complained she took credit which they thought should have been their's. They even suggested she should be sent off the field. How dare she take an entire day just to pray!

At a later time they confessed error in judgement and apologies were proffered, but for the duration of their greivance the waves they made lashed at team unity. Precious time and energy and thought went for naught. The mission itself could have been placed in jeopardy as they sought acknowledgement and accolades and the undermining of Mary Lou's efforts.

"Yes, pride is on every mission field. You have to get over that. I didn't have a problem with that (pride) because I wasn't that proud of myself."

Advice from Mary Lou: "Be sure to listen to the voice of the Lord and do what He says versus what people say."

"All bitterness, anger and wrath, insult
and slander must
be removed from you, along with all wickedness.
And be kind and compassionate to
one another, forgiving
one another, just as God also forgave you
in Christ."
Ephesians 4:31-32

Life Support

"Above all, fear the LORD and worship Him
faithfully with all your heart, considering the
great things He has done for you."
1 Samuel 12:24

When you sow amidst peoples who have
vastly different cultural and belief systems
you may, along with experiencing the potential
positives of the involvement, confront its potential dangers.

In 1982 a stranger paid Mary Lou what seemed,
at first, a social visit. His reason unquestioned, she
greeted him kindly and invited him in for coffee
and cake as she did everyone who dropped by.
They talked in a casual manner for awhile before
she learned his identity. He was the older brother
of Reshma, a young Indian who had recently
become a believer. She had left the Muslim faith
and was now a follower of Jesus.

Abruptly Reshma's brother changed his tone
and asked "Why did you change my sister?"

Little did Mary Lou know at that point what
his intention was but in reply she stated simply

"I cannot change anybody. Only God can change a person."

The knife he concealed was to be used to take Mary Lou's life.

She related honestly that she had shared Christ with Reshma and had given his sister the Gospel message. She explained she could do no less... and could do no more.

It was her initial response that disarmed her unusual visitor and resulted in her life being spared that day. He left her presence with new thoughts and Mary Lou never saw him again. Two weeks later Mary Lou learned from Reshma her brother had indeed purposed to kill her for the change he believed she had wrought upon his sister. That Mary Lou gave God the credit due, which was the natural course for her, was fault-less and fortuitous, as it was meant to be.

Much has been written on the subject of changing religions. In India, honor killings have taken place for centuries. Saving face is essential in the culture.

Indian Ways And Means

Believers Believing

How strongly do Indian believers believe? This tale certainly tells. It is told by N. J. Varughese, founder of 'All India Mission'.

"Over five hundred workers traveled by train or bus to reach Ranchi to attend our worker's conference. It was time to hear reports from the various fields. One report was from Pastor D. R. Nag from Orissa, regarding the persecution last year. He said 50,000 Christians fled from their villages, 1,500 churches were destroyed or damaged, 150 Christians were murdered... some even burned alive... and hundreds of Christian villages were completely leveled."

"Then he told us an amazing story about how elephants seem to be taking revenge against the persecutors."

(Editor's Note: Wild elephants can uproot trees, tear down houses, turn over buses, and easily kill people.)

"In Orissa herds of wild elephants have been coming out of the jungles and wrecking havoc on the villages where the worst offenses against

87

Christians occurred. This past August, one year to the day after Hindus attacked a certain village, a herd of elephants emerged from the surrounding jungle and destroyed a lot of the perpetrator's homes. Smaller elephants from the herd entered the village first, as if to survey, and then returned to the herd. Then the larger elephants entered the village. Such strange attacks have spread and more than 700 houses in 30 villages have been destroyed."

"Nobody in the area has seen or even imagined the unique appearance of a herd of wild elephants such as this. The elephants never attack Christians and the fear of God has fallen on the local people, who remember very well what they did to the Christians last year. Locals have labeled the participating elephants 'Christian elephants'."

"Until now the Lord has given us peace in Jharkland, but we all know of the terror that occurred in Orissa. I have noticed a shift in people's attitudes. Recently there have been indications that violence could erupt in our area, and people are living in genuine fear. A report from Brother Tiwari said many are coming to the Lord in his mission field, but that Hindus are stirring up trouble."

"After Brother Tiwari's report I got a little inspiration. I prayed the strangest prayer ever: I asked the Lord to send 50 wild elephants to Tiwari's village. I didn't ask for anybody to be harmed or for any property to be damaged. I simply asked the Lord to send a visual demonstration of His mighty power. I knew those who oppose the Gospel would understand the message. I also knew it would be an encouragement to our believers to see God's hand of protection on them. Our believers would also learn that God answers prayer... even when we ask for something unusual."

"A week later Pastor Tiwari called. Our conversation went something like this:"

"We're remembering your prayer!"

"Which prayer?"

"Your prayer for 50 wild elephants. They came!!"

"Really? Where did they come from?"

"Nobody knows. They just appeared. The God of Heaven sent 50 wild elephants because of your prayer."

"Details of the story are the elephants gathered in the fields surrounding Tiwari's village and our believers were expecting them because of my prayer and so they went immediately out and started counting them to make sure there were exactly 50. There were 44 grown elephants and 5 calves. Only 49 elephants."

"'Lord!' they cried. 'Our beloved pastor asked for 50 elephants! There are only 49 here! Where is the missing elephant?' They went to bed that night a little disturbed and confused about why the Lord didn't answer the prayer precisely."

"When they woke the next morning they discovered that one of the elephants had given birth. The newborn calf made up the difference. A small miracle."

"The elephants stayed near the village... completely peaceful, causing no disturbance whatsoever... until the Indian forestry officials came and 'persuaded' the elephants to return to the jungle. God truly answers prayer!"

Not My Job

Who does what in India... without any words spoken. As related by Al Lester, three term missionary to India (who also tells the two other shorts which follow).

"Five of us were driving in Behpotholedar. Two men and two women and myself. The women sitting in the back seat and three men in front. The driver stopped beside the steep slope of a hill where a quantity of down wood could be seen. Silently the two women exited the vehicle and climbed the hill a number of times, gathering branches and piling them in the back seat. The two men, their husbands, sat patiently while they did the work, doing nothing."

"The wood, which was very rough, was stacked solidly up to the level of the windows. I began to wonder how we would all get home... where we could all sit... when the ladies, again without communication of any sort, not even the wave of a hand, climbed in on top of the firewood. Without any buffer to protect them they held on for an hour and a half on the bouncy roads until our destination was reached."

And it isn't they don't love their wives. It's simply the culture and the way things get done... and by whom. Everyone understands their role and what is expected of them... and they just do it.

Indians Can See In The Dark

"Hitching a ride on the back of a speeding motorcycle being driven on the barely existing, potholed roads of India in the middle of the night...

without headlights. The headlights weren't just not turned on... they didn't exist. It was as if the driver had totally memorized the roads... bump by bump, rut by rut, washout by washout... in order for us to make our wreckless way as we were. Missing most of the obstacles... slamming into only a few."

Divine guidance?

Or, perhaps Indians can see in the dark!

Built In Obsolescence

"I've seen something similar to this on a number of occasions. There was a telephone booth standing there. You could see the wires, the cables, sticking up out of the top of it, ending there, unconnected to anything. You could see that the telephone was not working. But nobody cared about the fact it would not operate. It really did not need to work they said. What was important was the telephone booth was there. That it was owned."

"And there was a refrigerator which was not working. And it didn't matter that it was not working. What mattered was it was there. That someone had the status without the worry of future repairs or paying for electricity."

Materialism in check.

1955. "One of our regular patients came and asked for me. She told Timothy, our native personal worker, that she wanted me to come to her son's wedding. He explained the Fredericks were waiting for me but she insisted that I should come and bring Ruby with me. Just then I walked in and NO would not do. We said we could 'only stay for a very few minutes'. When we arrived we saw the bride and groom sitting on a specially made throne which was very highly decorated. The groom is the important person of the wedding and he was dressed in the best Indian jacket with a white turban trimmed in gold. The bride, who is very unimportant in the wedding, wore a rich shade of red. They both were decked with garlands made of flowers. We were given privileged seats right in front of the bride and groom. The bride's mother gave away the bride, signifying she would have nothing more to do with her affairs and the groom now had complete control of her. This ceremony takes about one half hour. The bride's mother makes all kinds of funny motions with her arms and sprinkles the bride and groom with rice, coconut milk and perfume. They presented Ruby and I with garlands. Because I was the guest of honor mine had three silver balls in it. They sprinkled perfume on us and then brought two silver plates with coconut, bananas, and beadle nut. We told them we had to leave, saving the embarrassing situation of not eating the food as we would not chew the beadle nut."

Also 1955. "We had a rap on the gate of our compound so Ruby went to answer it. She asked who it was and the voice said 'You must come to the munchie's (language teacher's) house right away'. Ruby asked if someone was sick but they said no but that we must come. I should tell you we usually do not venture out at night unless it is an emergency case. We got dressed and cautiously walked over to our munchie's house. It was just a stone throw away so we did not have to go far.

When we got there there were several people and they told us to come in. We entered, still cautious, and sat in the chairs they offered. We must have really looked scared as they laughed at us. Then our munchie walked in and I did look frightened then I'm sure because his eyes looked just as if he was demon possessed. He spoke and told us we had been invited over to the ceremony of the first cutting of the boy's hair. The priest of the Brahams goes through a ritual of prayer, etc., for the family to keep the evil demons away. Then we were given plantains and sugar and told we could make a move so we excused ourselves and said a polite namascara and left as quickly as we could. Oh, the life of a missionary."

1965-1967

"When I am in Myosore there is a continual stream of visitors. Saturday 17 women and children from my neighborhood came over to see me. It was a real opportunity to tell them about Christ. What was interesting is they didn't ask me where I was from, etc., but about the book they always see me reading... which is the Word of God. It shows they are watching. Pray my life will radiate Christ."

"I went again to Erode to lead meetings and training classes. During the six days I had thirty meetings in all. The Mission Hospital staff and also the government hospital nurses, including the Hindu nurses, attended as did the Nursing Superintendent. God spoke, the Spirit convicted, and the Lord's Word did not return unto Him void."

"The Nilgiris retreat was blessed by the Lord and eight of the girls were drawn to Him and are now His children. It was a joy to see how the Lord used those who came last year in sending more to the retreat this year."

"The tribal work continues to be a blessing. The last dispensary day Dr. Herlufsen was unable to come so I had to carry on. With the able assistance of the workers in that area we were able to see 123 patients."

"When I came home Saturday night someone had stolen my electric meter so I am without electricity. The electric department won't do anything. I have to get a contractor to get it replaced."

"My Dear Auntie. Needless to say your letter was a great shock to me. There was no time earlier to read post so I set it aside til I went to bed. I am glad I was alone and it was quiet. My thoughts and prayers are with you. I know it must be very lonesome for you but I do praise the Lord with you that He was gracious to take Uncle without days of suffering. The Lord is your strength and comfort in these days I know. If ever you feel you need me I will take an emergency furlough."

"Florence wrote to tell me Betty Thompson went to be with the Lord. Also my second grade teacher, Miss Fisher, wrote. She had been to see Betty twice the week before. The second time she had had a heart attack."

"In the hospital we have a girl and the people of her village just can't understand why they can't be with her. We give her sedatives and then they shake her and disturb her again. Just before we left we sent them all home. I went down just now and 27 were all around her shaking her."

"Now you know I have had trouble with my extension to stay in India. It has been due to my extensive travel so the police advise I go someplace and stay put."

Not More Than You Can Bear

Astonishingly Mary Lou was completely free from any major bodily injury the entire three and a half decades she ministered in India. A remarkable account. An awesome hedge. She does not even remember a stubbed toe. Once she fell fifteen or so feet off a wall, did a backward half somersault in air, and landed on her feet.

Illness, however, was a different matter... a monster rearing its ugly head many, many times. Mary Lou suffered malaria so often over thirty-four years keeping a tally was early on abandoned. Once, in Switzerland, "The whole chateau shook from my chills!" In recalling that episode Mary Lou chuckled.

And it was from Switzerland that her insulin came. A virus had destroyed the natural insulin in her pancreas about 1982 (being diagnosed in 1986) and the medication available in India was ineffective against her stage of diabetes. She worked seven years in the field while managing the disease. She also endured adhesions from amoebic dysentary.

"Another time I had severe pain and the doctors and I thought I had appendicitis, but when they gave me the anesthesia for the surgery to remove the appendix, I passed bladder stones. Then another time I was sick a long time with hepatitus when I went to Bangolore. I stayed in the YWCA and the doctors treated me there because they did not want me in the hospital for fear that others would catch it."

Mary Lou is living proof positive following Christ does not make life a bed of roses. There is a price paid in service too.

"For fifteen days I have had terrible pain. It seems a nerve has been damaged in dental work. I keep praising the Lord and ask Him to keep me smiling and full of His joy but alone in my room I scream. Is it wrong? Do you do the same? I feel bad when I do scream with pain as I am sure it's not nearly as bad as our Lord suffered. I am thankful for the little the Lord has allowed me to suffer for then I can sympathize better with others who suffer. May He be glorified in our suffering."

What all did Mary Lou 'catch' and endure over the 3.6 decades in India? In alphabetical order:

amoebic dysentary
bladder stones
colds, colds, colds
colitis
diabetes
gastritis (severe)
hepatitis
hives (severe)
influenza (severe)
kidney infection
kidney stones

malaria (untold times)
rabies injections (bitten by dogs)
toothache (nerve damage)
water on the knee

Trials
Reshma Ahmed
(A Christ Follower in the School of Trials)

"Trials are the bedrock of any Christian's growth. Knowing Christ for the first time and facing trials for the first time after knowing Christ can generate emotions on either end of the spectrum. While the former is the most surreal experience that lights the core of one's being, the latter can dim and put out the light in no time."

"My experience as a novice believer was typical of the above, but God in His wisdom, knew better and prepared me in the school of trials to quickly mature me from a baby Christian to a young adult Christian, whose foundation is now rooted in Christ Jesus alone."

"Trials can be long-lasting, painful, shaking, eroding, devastating and even deadly, if not taken in the right perspective, seeking counsel from the Lord, dwelling in the Word of God, waiting, praying and being thankful! The last action is most powerful that binds all the strategies together to create the miracle God wants to do in your life. Consider trials to be like an advanced, condensed, academic course that bestows you a degree in half the amount of time required to graduate."

"Trials help one graduate summa cum laude on the path of being a Christ follower. It grows you immensely, in a very short amount of time and permanently to be the person God had intended you to be. As it says in James 1:2-4:

Consider it pure joy, my brothers, whenever you
face trials
of many kinds, because you know that the
testing of your
faith develops perseverance. Perseverance must
finish its work
so that you may be mature and complete, not
lacking anything.

"This type of learning is immune to the ravages of time or the aging process. Therefore, such a person puts on Godly traits at a fast and furious rate to be that changed soul created in the image of God. As it says in Ephesians 4:22-24:

You were taught, with regard to your former way
of life, to put
off your old self, which is being corrupted by its
deceitful desires;
to be made new in the attitude of your minds;
and to put on the
new self, created to be like God in true
righteousness and holiness.

Mary Lou posing with one of the girls.

Lissyamma Kurian in a period photograph.

Reshma Ahmed and her children in a fairly recent photograph.

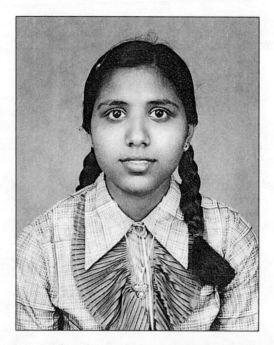

**Annamma Abraham in a period photograph.
Once in Mary Lou's Sunday School in
Bangalore, now teaching Bible.**

Adeline Barber and family in 1988.

**Mary Lou with nurses from the North India
Hospital all dressed in saris.**

Mary Lou with graduate nurses.

Wedding bells for Ed and Mary Lou.

Out Of India

The missionary William Carey labored forty-one years in India. He never returned to England.

The missionary Mother Teresa labored sixty-six years in India. She never saw her mother again.

The missionary Mary Lou Loucks labored thirty-six years in India. She furloughed back to the U. S. of A. four times, only returning when there was cause, never due to a sabbatical being due. Her first respite came after seven years and its purpose was twofold. She was assigned to care for her future husband's first wife (more on this in a later chapter) while Mrs. Frederick was ill and hospitalized. And it was the year Mary Lou studied for and earned her Bachelor's Degree in Nursing at Empire State College. She did so well she was asked to stay on and continue for her Master's. Mary Lou informed them she had to turn back to India for her Master but agreed with them she could study there and show up in future for the degree. Which she did. On her second big break, which lasted nine months, she acquired her Master's of Education in Nursing and, impressively, completed her PhD theory in Cardiology Nursing. She did not do her dissertation, so no

Doctor of Philosophy Degree was ever awarded. Her work always came first.

"After I earned my Bachelor's and Master's degrees I went back to India, to Bangalore to live. While I was there I worked at Muslim hospitals, Hindu hospitals, government hospitals, and Christian hospitals. I went to these hospitals to teach nursing and Bible. During this time I taught courses in cardiology in continuing education for nurses and doctors in Bangalore and also in northern India. I taught these courses for six weeks at a time in each hospital and then I moved on to the next hospital. I taught all over India from the north to the south to the east to the west. I also taught in some of the universities where they had nursing programs. When I had these courses, I had different people come in to teach about leprosy, trauma, and orthopedics. At this time there were doctors and nurses coming from the US, Europe, Indonesia, and, of course, India."

Once Mary Lou had finished her Master's Degree she was able to teach more cardiology than she had before. Teaching cardiology was her 'foot in the door' at many hospitals throughout India. Always she made the agreement with them that she would teach cardiology only if they let her teach Bible studies right alongside.

Through her medical connections Mary Lou was invited to Switzerland on a number of occasions. All expenses were paid in exchange for knowledge in nursing and cardiology she had garnered over the years... and was willing to share. Medical practitioners and educators filled auditoriums and halls to hear her and be enlightened.

Swiss doctors and hospitals bade her return often to speak.

And Mary Lou did return often, traveling far and wide on God's errands. Things did not always go smoothly. On Mary Lou's Atlantic crossing aboard the ship 'United States' 999 out of 1,000 persons were seasick, some for the entire voyage. Only one man was known to make all meals. Things did not always go quickly. Later trips on aircraft were 150 times faster than those aboard the Queen Elizabeth and the Britannic.

Gandhi And Teresa

So I prefaced my question with "All the thirty-six years you were in India Mother Teresa was in country also." My hope of course was that she had met her. "Did you ever meet her?"

"Oh, yes. We were good friends."

Suddenly it dawned on me I would have to ask very specific questions to elicit very pertinent responses. Perhaps the first thing most people would proclaim was they were good friends with Mother Teresa (or that they had even seen the woman). But the fact was drawn out finally during our fourth formal interview. Mary Lou is not one to name drop... well, with the one exception, that of Jesus. She certainly does not boast of herself.

At one point Mother Teresa made a special request of Mary Lou Loucks. She wanted Mary Lou to take over the medical work of a group of mentally ill Indian children, which she was willing to do. After arriving on scene, however, Mary Lou was aghast at the extremely poor conditions under which they were forced to live. Everything the children possessed at one time had been sold for a few rupees by their supposed caregivers. Even the very mattresses which would have kept

111

them from sleeping on cold concrete. The children suffered mightily from colds and rheumatic pain. So neglected had they been Mary Lou closed the facility and returned with the children by train to Calcutta for what could only be better treatment.

At other times Mary Lou and Mother Teresa got together for tea and chat... comparing notes and sharing thoughts on the state of India. They often prayed together.

I asked "Did you agree on most things discussed or did you have opposite views?"

"I was very careful with what I said in our talks but Mother Teresa was a wonderful Christian. She was even kicked out of the Catholic church for being too Christian. When she became well known they took her back."

(Note of interest: Mother Teresa was born
Agnese Gonxhe Bojaxhiu
to Albanian parents and grew up in
Skopje, Macedonia.)

Five years before Mary Lou arrived in India Mahatma Gandhi was assassinated. In 1984 Indira Gandhi, Ranjiv Gandhi's mother, was also assassinated (by her own bodyguards). Ranjiv Gandhi became the seventh Prime Minister of India.

(Note of interest: Mahatma Gandhi
and Indira Gandhi were not related.)

Somehow Mary Lou's experience and expertise leaked to the government and Ranjiv Gandhi was compelled to contact her for the sake of the Indian people. He asked that she teach medical care and techniques to many native practitioners. Mary Lou was pleased to share knowledge... with her one, standard condition.

To this Ranjiv Gandhi gave his personal permission and good nursing and Good News shared a remarkable stage. A medical ministry miracle.

"Around 1988 Ranjiv Ghandi wrote a letter requesting me to teach cardiology in the central government hospitals. These were different from the government hospitals that were run locally. They were run directly by the central government. I gave him the same stipulation I gave others. I would only teach cardiology if they let me teach Bible as well. He granted my request and while I was in these hospitals, they always provided a car for me, gave me lovely rooms to stay in, sometimes in hotels, and gave me many gifts because I would not take any money for this. Many Bible studies were established in these hospitals, and the doctors and nurses went on to bring Bible studies into other central government hospitals."

"During the last period of my work in India I had a new base hospital called Odachatdrum. It was a Christian hospital, started by Indian doctors. They did not normally want missionary doctors working there because they wanted to keep the staff homogeneous. However, they made an exception with me. They asked me to come and work there. They liked me so much they asked me to stay and offered me a place to live and retire."

1968-1970

"**I** am just getting over another attack of malaria. Not as bad as the one in November and the one in December. Trust it is getting out of my system again. It had been out for several years but apparently during my October trip I was bit again and contracted a very severe type. Now I feel good but worn out so I was ordered to another day's rest. I worked with it till yesterday noon but had to give in then."

"Many have asked if I have the freedom to witness here. Please make it clear that that is one of the main reasons I am here. I have the liberty to give the Gospel to everyone. Patients and staff as well as anyone else I contact in any way."

"If an eye doctor came they would get plenty of experience and see many eye diseases that they could never see in America."

"Dr. Samuel's sister-in-law said they have some kind of diapers in America that dry up so the baby does not get chilled at night. Do you know anything about them? If so she would like a dozen sent out by air."

"Today we have been busy with an 18 year old girl who fell in a well. She is fortunate to be alive.

Broke only her fibia and tibia just above the ankle. Scraped her arm and hit her head. But is fine."

"A group of us went to the gov't hospital in Ooty on Friday for a Bible study. Several girls came to the meeting with Hindu caste marks so I thought they were Hindu. So I said 'seeing there are so many Hindu girls here this evening I would like to get your view of who you think Jesus is'. I was really shocked when they said they weren't Hindu but Christian. In the hospital they are not willing to be identified as Christians."

"Yes, it really seems America needs missionaries, or I should say Christ, more than any country these days. My heart ached when we got word of the assassination of Dr. King."

"We have been without electricity in the hospital for four days. We are having a very bad monsoon or cyclone. Trees are down and roofs of some of our buildings have been blown off. Doors have been split right off with the hinges and part of the door left on. Windows blown out. But life goes on. Babies keep coming."

"I saw the first hippies last evening. I had heard about them but could never imagine what they were really like. India seems to be getting a flood of them from other countries and it really is a disgrace. How can our Lord tarry? His coming must be at hand."

Most Fearful

Mary Lou had plenty of reasons to be afraid in India but she was fearless. Or at least seemed fearless. Doing her job and what was right... at times just being fair and principled... placed her in harm's way way too often. There were attempts upon her life.

"Sometimes I ran across dishonest workers at Kotagiri. One time in specific, a house was being built for an eye specialist that was to join the staff. I happened to notice that they were not using the iron rods they said they were for the construction of the ceiling. So I quietly snuck in and took some pictures and presented them to the committee. The workers were reprimanded even though they were high up on the totem pole. They of course did not like this and tried to kill me. They put large rocks across the road once when I was driving. The road was an ascending hill, so naturally I would have stepped on the gas to get up the grade. But the Lord told me just in time to slow down before I ran into them. Sure enough, there the rocks were, that I would have crashed into, across the mud road." They believed she would be crushed in her vehicle.

"This was not the only time the Lord protected my life. I was very observant and honest in my work there. There were many times when I had to expose dishonest actions among the hospital workers. One time some of the workers set my room on fire. Thank the Lord, I had gone up to the doctor's house. The men who did it, did not know this of course." They believed they would be burning her to death.

"One time I was teaching at a Muslim hospital near my own home. Every day I walked to the hospital and back again. One day some children started throwing stones at me. This went on for three or four days. One stone hit me on the spine and I was a bit concerned about this. I reported it to the hospital authorities and told them that unless this stopped I would be afraid to come for fear of injury. They notified the police. The police in plain dress would be on guard as I walked back and forth. After a week I asked some of the nurses if they would like to walk with me back home and they happily did so. We met some of these children and I asked the nurses to ask the children why they were throwing stones at me. They said it was because their parents told them to do so because I was teaching about Jesus in their hospital. So I invited the children to my home and gave them cookies, cake, and pop and told them about Jesus. From then on the children came regularly to my home at least two or three times a week and before I finished the course in the hospital, they had all come to the Lord! They continued to visit me after I left the hospital whenever I was in town." They believed they could thwart

God's plans by having their children cast stones at Mary Lou.

"Another time, when going to the hospitals, I was bitten by two dogs. I had to take rabies injections and when I went to get them locally I noted that they were going to use a needle that they had already given to somebody else, so I refused to take it there. I took an eight hour journey up to Coonoor, to the Pasteur Insitute, where they made various vaccines, and asked them if they would supply me with the injections to take home and give to myself. They consented and all was fine." Satan thought dogs would accomplish what those in league with him did not achieve.

Another common danger, not necessarily life threatening, was theft. At one point, while in Kotagiri, Mary Lou hired on a married man and woman to help with the overload of chores. Unfortunately, not satisfied with that employment and their improved income, they took advantage of familiarity and broke in when they knew Mary Lou was away, and stole many of her belongings.

Reshma Ahmed

Eight years before Mary Lou returned from the India mission fields Reshma Ahmed, a sixteen year old Muslim girl, met her. Mary Lou's sharing and caring, along with that of other Christians, turned Reshma's search for answers and hope toward Jesus. In an initial reaction to her new faith her family locked Reshma in her room for a full year... only feeding her... not speaking to her... and allowed her to see no one. These few questions and Reshma's responses sum up her remembrances... and reveal a deep regard for Mary Lou. It was Reshma's older brother who intended to kill Mary Lou for 'changing' his sister.

What are your memories of Mary Lou in India?
"Aunty Mary Lou had a radiant smile that lit up a room and all the people in it like no other I have known so far in my life. There was this light that came from within which was unquenchable no matter how strained a situation could turn."

"She was an excellent baker, and made the most wonderful cakes and cookies I had tasted as a child or while living in Bangalore. Growing up, cake was a rarity and a delicacy because in India we rarely baked due to power outages, so Aunty's cakes and desserts were really a knockout."

Of course Mary Lou knew all about baking from her deli days. She was well known and well liked for her chocolate cakes (she baked up to fifteen of them a day) and her cinnamon breads.

"Aunty Mary Lou was genuine, hospitable and so compassionate that it was very difficult to dismiss her or not be affected by her actions. She was the Lord's hands and feet which melted even the hardest of hearts."

How did you hear the Good News and come to faith?

"I was seventeen years of age. God placed me in the company of Christians—'Believers' whose hallmark was 'Faith in Action'. I was attracted by their unique friendliness, selfless and helpful actions, the God they represented was more like a friend—one to be cherished rather than feared. I heard the Good News and saw it in action, followed by hymns and songs, and then finally, when I called upon Jesus in my hour of need and desperation, He came down personally to fulfill that need and then there was no proof required. I followed His lead."

What did your own family think?

"My family was very upset, which was natural. They could have killed me but my father was a more liberal Muslim and did not believe in honor killing. When they realized that I was not going to turn back my father instituted the condition that I was to keep my change of faith a secret for a good reason. Because my older sisters were of marriageable age and if the word got out that I had changed my faith and had become a Christian it would have brought a lot of disgrace to my family and my sisters wouldn't have received any marriage proposals. So while their reaction was normal it nevertheless stunted my growth... but through such trials my character was also strengthened."

"While I lived with my family, there ensued a strained atmosphere because I was no longer practicing the Muslim faith as the entire family was. I was different, deviant, and of course not really a part of the same family anymore. Although we all lived together the binding force in the relationship was broken forever."

Your impressions of how severe the religious climate is for Christians in India today?

"The same as everywhere because Christians trying to follow Christ face all kinds of challenges. In some places the challenges may be very explicit and a matter of life and death whereas in other places the challenges may be more implicit, causing attrition slowly but surely. Within India itself, there is great diversity in the level and intensity of challenges depending upon the location. South India is more predominantly Christian than north India. That is because Christianity spread through the southern parts of India, due to coastal locations as missionaries traveled from the seas settling in south India and then migrating northwards."

Compared to years ago?

"Years ago the situation was not as bad because the media did not polarize situations or readily transmit the stories as it does now. It works both ways. Now there is more availability of the Good News but the caveat is that there is also the potential of mulitplying the adverse effects."

What led you to the United States?

"My oldest brother (who confronted Mary Lou) had come to the States as a graduate student and wanted to stay after completing his MS in Engineering. Most of my extended relatives had immigrated to the US and my family was looking to do the same. Without a close blood relative to sponsor us, we thought that if a few of us went as students and stayed back, we could then sponsor the rest of the family. In that pursuit, I too was accepted into a graduate program at the University of Tennessee at Knoxville and so came to the States. I now work in the mental health field."

Have you kept in touch with Mary Lou?

"Yes, I love her very much and have kept in touch with her since I found out her whereabouts. She is a dear sweetheart whose life reflects the work of Christ more completely and radiantly than I have seen in anybody else in my entire life!"

Another young Indian woman, Susy Mathew (now living down under) crossed Mary Lou's path about the same time. Her answers to similar questions revealed a different trail.

"Yes I have known Mary Lou for years, since 1982. I first met Mary Lou in India when I went to Bangalore, India for pre university studies. She ran a Bible study in the local church, Emmanuel Church, as well as in her home after church services. I remem- ber the joy of staying with her once for a week and studying Revelation. That was lots of fun. I enjoyed my stay in Bangalore. I had Mary Lou who helped me much with my Bible study as well as good Christian friends in the hostel where I stayed. Later I moved to Kerala to study medicine."

"I heard about the Lord when I was 16 years old and my older brother shared the Gospel with me. I must say that it stopped with accepting the Lord and it was in Bangalore that I grew closer to the Lord."

"My father used to make us read about all religions when we grew up. My father, being a Canaanite, also made us read about Israel and children growing up in that land. So it was just a matter of accepting the Lord and moving closer to Him. But it was with Mary Lou that I learned a deeper understanding of His Word and became grounded on His Word. This helped me soon after as I was the missions secretary of the evangelical union in Kerala as well as the president in the years 1985-1986-1987."

(Editor's Note: The Union of Evangelical Students of India (UESI) is a well established organization which involves students.)

"Reshma was in the same hostel (the Ursuline Hostel, Cooke town Karnataka State) that I lived in and I enjoyed daily time of praise and worship with her. 7 p.m. every day for almost two years. I do keep in touch with Reshma off and on. I do also keep in touch with Mary Lou, but much more often. There are weeks when we have met as much as three times on the phone to pray together."

Susy Mathew was born in Malaysia as was her future husband. Even though both of their families knew each other before they were born Susy did not meet Mr. Mathew in Malaysia. Nor did she meet him in Bangalore although he was there as well. That occurred in the far-flung land of Australia where Susy journeyed to train in psychiatry in 2002. They were married four years later, but not without a hitch...

"My father fell ill just before my wedding and so he could not travel to Australia. Seeing that Dad was unwell my mother refused to come with me as she would have had to travel back to Malaysia alone after the wedding. When Mary Lou heard this she came to Australia and stood in place of Mum."

Lissyamma Kurian. "I met Mary Lou in 1978 when I was a first year nursing student at Bangalore, India where she was a Christian missionary. I knew her as a good and dedicated teacher. She taught Bible classes in every nursing college and other educational centers like medical and dental colleges. Also, she conducted Bible classes at her house for anyone who reached her house. When I met her she was head nurse in one of the leprosy units at the hospital where I took nursing. The fact surprised me she was able to take care of those lepers with all love and affection in very limited facilities, with no advanced technologies, and not even a pair of gloves. The working atmosphere was a challenge to everyone and those patients where considered untouchable by their own relatives and natives, including me. When I asked her how she could do those jobs she said, 'Christ has done it and He can heal them. I am just taking care of them.' I believe she was working 16 hours a day to meet her work load. She witnessed of Christ in her deeds to all the nurses and nursing students."

"Since we all stayed in our nursing school dormitory, we loved to go to her house to enjoy her homemade food. Mary Lou was a very good cook and she made an abundance of food to feed us. There were several occasions where she cooked in big pots and pans for 50 people and served us in public gardens, because her little house couldn't accommodate us. I am always thankful to her for her special chocolate cakes (my favorite) and donuts which were delicacies for us in those days. And also she did her cooking alone, without any help, and we were not aware of the financial struggle it took to feed us. I feel sorry now I never helped her or never bothered to know how she did that. All her Bible classes ended up with a donut party (donuts were a rare item, not available in shops)."

"Though I was born and brought up in a Christian family I was blessed to learn the Word of God from Mary Lou. I knew a lot of Hindus and Muslims who came to know Christ through her."

"When I graduated in 1982 I left for Saudi Arabia looking for opportunity and did not have any contact with Mary Lou until I reached the USA on a nursing job visa in 1989. With my husband and my three children we visited her in 2002. She was married to Frederick who had

Alzheimer's disease. She was dedicated in taking care of him. After her husband passed away I was blessed to have her company in our house and am privileged to visit her often now because we live nearby."

Adeline Barber met Mary Lou in 1979. "I was doing my nurses training at St. Martha's School Of Nursing. I took a class about cardiac arrhythmias which she taught. Mary Lou prayed before the class and I had never heard anyone pray like that before. I was Catholic, went to mass daily and prayed but Mary Lou sounded like she had a relationship with Jesus. After class she invited all the nurses to her house for prayer and Bible study. Some of us began to go to her house. We would pray and have a snack and then she would do a Bible study. One time we did not see any food and right after she prayed and thanked God for the food someone knocked at the door and brought a tray of pastries. This was the first miracle that I saw. For the next couple of years I attended the Bible studies. I watched Hindus and Muslims give their hearts to Jesus and I watched Mary Lou disciple us."

"Mary Lou was unlike other missionaries. She did not try to make us adapt to her culture. We teased her about being more Indian than we were. She dressed like us, cooked our food and even spoke several of our languages. She was meticulous in not doing anything, going anywhere or saying anything which might discredit her witness. She not only showed genuine interest in the people who attended the Bible studies but she also visited our families. Mary Lou visited my home and was a friend to my entire family. She always prayed for needs and sent cards and letters. With all the people whose lives she touched over the years I do not know how she kept up with her correspondence. Every letter was hand written and every card personalized."

"On a more personal note: I came to the States to attend Bible School. While I was here I met a young man and wrote home to ask my parents for permission to get married. My parents were very apprehensive as they had not met him; he was American and not Catholic. Because they knew Mary Lou and had a relationship with her they asked her to meet him when she was in the States on vacation. Despite her busy schedule she came to visit and after she made sure he loved Jesus she gave my parents her opinion. My parents subsequently approved and we have been happily married for 25 years and serving the Lord."

"Mary Lou gave her life to Jesus and came to India. In spite of the huge cultural diversity she did everything she could to understand and assimilate the culture. She lived a life of a disciple in prayer, reading the Word, and Bible studies. Over the course of her tenure in India I cannot number the people she discipled."

So many like Reshma, Susy, Lissyamma, and Adeline, though their individual life stories vary greatly, need to know a Mary Lou. Well, need to know the Jesus in a Mary Lou.

Preparing The Way

M ary Lou lived an incredibly difficult and painful childhood no matter what comparisons are made. She endured trauma at age five, her father's rage and rejection at nine, and the death of her mother from cancer at thirteen. She learned about being poor and at age ten, smack in the middle of the Great Depression, she was putting in twenty hour days to cover her simple room and board. It could be argued it all served her well.

It taught her to be self-reliant when she needed to be. To be studious on her own... from kindergarten... and become self-educated.

It granted her the ability to endure pain and recognize and acknowledge the pain of others. And to fathom, at a deep level, the spurning and treatment converts to Christianity received from their families.

It revealed to her the very real healing prowess and miracles of God. Led her toward compassion and forgiveness. Drew out qualities allowing her to be calm in the midst of storm and ever patient under dire circumstance.

Mary Lou learned to ask the Lord for His guidance and strength and wisdom, so often requisite.

The many trials and occasional triumphs of her upbringing, the tests and tears of her childhood, prepared her for adult ministry to come... to be hands and feet. In the place called India.

So Overcome

So I asked Mary Lou one of my toughest questions. "Did you ever see your father face to face again after he threw you out of the family at age nine?"

"Four or five times. Always in the distance."

I paused so she continued "After I went to India I wrote him a letter each week. For twenty years I wrote him... every week."

I said "What?"

And Mary Lou repeated "After I went..."

So I asked "Did he ever write back?"

"No, never did."

So, keeping to my notes, I asked my next even tougher question. "Were you able to forgive your father?"

"I didn't need to forgive him. I never held any grudge against him. After I was in India for twenty years, on one of my return trips, I went out to California where he had moved and visited my father. With tears streaming down his face he asked me why I, the one he had rejected and thrown away, could be the one who cared about him now." His other two children, who he had done much for, were not even in contact with him. Mary Lou's answer to him was "God gave me a love for you. You sent me out because it was God's will. I needed to be on my own. This was the plan for my life."

Before his death Mary Lou's father became a Christian.

Well, Hello Mary Lou

1952. "Thank you for your letter of Nov. 18 addressed to Mr. Frederick. He is in India now and has been for four years. Mary Lou shall join him as soon as the Lord permits."

1989. Little did Mary Lou realize what was in store for her. She had remained busily single her sixty-three years and matrimony no longer seemed on the horizon. It wasn't that she wasn't a catch. A number of suitors (five prior to and four in India by actual count) had asked for her hand over those years and she had refused the entire lot. She was married to her work, if you will, after all. She had recently departed India but not her passion. In love with Jesus was she.

Mr. Frederick became the General Director of 'India Mission' in the early 1950's and suggested its name be changed to 'International Missions, Inc.' which was voted on and in. He was at that time Mary Lou's boss. "I worked alongside him and his first wife on the mission field for two years when I first started in India. I had met them about five years back when they came to my Bible school in Buffalo to speak. I didn't know we would later be working in the same mission until we all arrived in India. It's a small world and God indeed knows what He is doing."

Flash forward thirty-some years. Olive, Mr. Frederick's first wife, died of ovarian cancer in 1989. After that he began to write letters to Mary Lou. Initially he wrote about Olive. Then he began to write about marriage in general. He started asking Mary Lou questions relative to her thoughts about marriage. She thought nothing of it, that he wanted a shoulder to cry on. "There were several women interested in him, why would he ever think of me? Besides, I was almost 65 and my mind was not on marriage. I gave that up to the Lord a long time ago."

"In January of 1990, I flew to Los Angeles for a job interview. Some American doctors had written to me in India, asking me to come and work and teach in their hospital. It would have been a good position, paying $60,000 a year, plus housing, utilities, and an annual trip to India. When I arrived I told them I would accept the job if they would allow me to teach the Gospel. They said 'no', so I declined the position."

"While I was there Ed contacted me through a friend, asking if he could see me." Mary Lou, though once in her life clueless, said "Sure". When they met he proclaimed the desire to wed and exclaimed "God has told me I should marry you Mary Lou!"

Her immediate response was somewhat curt: "Really? Well, He hasn't told me!"

"I told Ed I would consider it in prayer. Two days later the Lord showed me in His Word that I was to marry him. I was not in love with him. I wasn't even attracted to him. I found it hard to say yes, but when the Lord tells you to do something, you do it. So I obeyed."

"I did say 'only if it was okay with all the daughters'."

"Ed asked me again on a Wednesday, we drove up to Arroyo Grande where he lived, we bought the cake and our license, I spoke at a Bible class at his church at his request, and the following Sunday we were married."

On January 7th they knotted in a private ceremony with a few members of family and friends present. Mary Lou wore a dress she had owned for fifteen years. Her brother gave her away.

Pastor Burke had been a little hesitant in performing the rites since never had he done so without thorough marital consultation beforehand. Somehow he felt it really wasn't necessary this occasion, and agreed to the exception.

What Mary Lou did do with "I do" was impressive. She instantly acquired (was blessed with) five daughters, five sons-in-law, seventeen grandchildren, and twenty-three great-grandchildren.

"But from eternity to eternity the LORD's
faithful love is
toward those who fear Him, and His
righteousness toward
the grandchildren of those who keep His
covenant, who
remember to observe His instructions."
Psalm 103:17-18

The couple honeymooned for two days on the Pacific Coast (and two years later second honeymooned to Canada and Niagara Falls).

Twenty days post wedding Mary Lou returned to India one last time. She spent her final weeks in country setting up Christian libraries in three separate hospitals.

"We had marital bliss for 15 years, 10 months, and 4 days. Ed said to me several times every day 'I love you soooo much'."

At Ed's passing Mary Lou posted four hundred letters announcing his home going... and received more than four hundred in response.

4 x 6 Glossies

"I give thanks to my God for every
remembrance of you,
always praying with joy for all of you in
my every prayer,
because of your partnership in the Gospel from
the first day until now.
I am sure of this, that He who started a good
work in you will
carry it on to completion until the day
of Christ Jesus."
Philippians 1:3-6

A marvelous change is taking place in the lives of many of the folk who are Mary Lou's neighbors. Within her residential park, radiating from her home, is a burgeoning community. They have seen and heard the irresistible Jesus in the immoveable Mary Lou. They are coming to faith. One 93 year old woman. Another, 80 years of age, received Christ. 73 years. In 'Sunrise Village' being born again has no age limits.

These people are no doubt among the many persons pictured prominently throughout Mary Lou's home. She has photographs everywhere.

Not just shut away in a stack of picture albums. All about the walls and shelves and furniture... there as a constant reminder. Not to pray, but to bring to mind all those she specificly prays for... intercedes for. Many Mary Lou knew in India are there. Many more recently met are there. Now even this writer and his wife Linda are there.

And some of the local elementary and high schools heard of her reputation and work in India and asked Mary Lou to come and speak about Hinduism. "I said I would as long as I could give a comparative lecture on Christianity. They agreed and I was able to give the Gospel to many children."

Even in America... a vast mission field.

Never Ending Story

The Reverend Dr. Paul E. Toms served Park Street Church in Boston, Massachusetts for twenty-five years. A past president of the National Association of Evangelicals, Dr. Toms also served as Chairman of the World Relief Corporation for 15 years. He has traveled and ministered over much of the world. He holds degrees from Fuller Theological Seminary and Gordon-Conwell Theological Seminary. He has authored articles for journals and papers, and produced the book, Winning the Battles of Life which enjoyed many printings and translation into Chinese.

"The Scripture describes a visit our Lord made one time to a home of friends. He taught sacred truths, and one of the sisters complained that no one, particularly her sister Mary, seemed willing to help in the preparations that had to be made. Jesus replied to her, "Mary has chosen what is better". I often have thought this describes another Mary I know... Mary Lou Frederick."

"My wife and I have known Mary Lou for many years, and the distinct impression is that she has made every effort over her entire life to choose what is better in order to obey and honor the Lord. She trusted Him to guide her in those many years of devoted service in India. She was committed to the Biblical understanding of the place of Missions in the believers life. She faithfully prayed and trusted the Savior to guide and provide. She chose the better things. And the Lord has graciously honored this obedience in so many ways. And as the years have rolled by, she has never wavered in her devotion. Even now, while many would rightfully feel it is time to sit back and rest a bit, Mary Lou keeps on choosing to serve the Lord. I know a bit about how many hills she has walked in her neighborhood in order to help people, to pray with people, to teach Bible classes. She attends meetings, she travels over our country to speak and teach, she is busy all the time. When she is ill, she can hardly wait to be well so she can get back to serving the Lord. This is a lady who has spent her life choosing what is better in order to lift up the name of our great Redeemer. No one will ever know, including Mary Lou, how many times she has answered the phone, gone to a house, prayed with someone, attended a missions meeting, witnessed to the truth of the Gospel, written letters and Bible studies, and just constantly expressed love for Christ our Savior. She has honored Him by choosing the better things."

Paul Toms

Passing The Flame

"**I** am pleased to say a word of encouragement relating to the absolute necessity of the work of the Gospel being passed on to others in order that it may have a hearing around the world."

"All the Biblical books and sermons and teachings about Missions come into focus here. I shall not try to repeat this material. I would point out to you that the Apostle had some clearly understood things to say about our responsibilities. For example, read the 5th chapter of 2 Corinthians. Notice verse 18 and see how he tells us that the ministry of reconciliation has been committed to us, and therefore we are Christ's ambassadors. That clearly implies a responsibility and we are to obey. Again, one of my favorite passages is found in 2 Timothy 2:2. Paul clearly instructs us to take the things we have heard and share them with others, so that the news may get out around the world. Other translations indicate we are to hand these things on. This has been the New Testament pattern. Learn, accept, understand, and tell others, or give to others as an entrusted deposit to be shared around the world. We all get old, we all become limited in what we can do. It is so important that others take our place. People come and go, churches come and go, God chooses some to be leaders and founders, and he chooses others to carry on. The work goes on, and it is done, as always, by loyal, obedient people who listen for God's voice and then obey."

Paul Toms

'Passing The Flame'. The title and theme of a recent missions conference at Mary Lou's home church, Grace Bible. She shared the platform and her heart with an attentive audience, and bade them heed the world around them and the need of all peoples. Not only addressing their physical needs. Not only feeding them or getting them clean water. Not only giving medical care. Not just saving their lives. Saving their souls.

Make no mistake, Mary Lou is all over others, young and old and in-between, joining in God's good work on myriad mission fields. That's all over as in fully encouraging... not all over as in done. Though older now, well... 84, the race Mary Lou is running has not ended. 'Sharing The Flame'... in Mary Lou's case... is perhaps much more apropos.

In fact, I have it on good authority that Mary Lou's story does not end with Mary Lou. Though she herself... as are we all... an earthly vapor, her story... the story of Jesus in her... is eternal.

LaVergne, TN USA
29 June 2010
187715LV00002B/1/P